THE WORLD OF BRENDAN BEHAN

The World of
Brendan Behan

edited by
SEAN McCANN

Drawings by LIAM C. MARTIN

A FOUR SQUARE BOOK

© Copyright by New English Library Limited 1965

*

First published by The New English Library Limited in November 1965

*Four Square Books are published by The New English Library Limited, from Barnard's Inn, Holborn, London, E.C.1
Made and printed in Great Britain by C. Nicholls & Company Ltd.*

ACKNOWLEDGEMENTS

The Editor wishes to thank the following for permission to reproduce copyright material: Messrs. Hutchinson & Company Limited for extracts from 'Borstal Boy', and Messrs. Methuen & Company Limited for passages from 'The Quare Fellow', both by Brendan Behan.

THE EDITOR

Sean McCann, who edited this collection, is thirty-five. At present features editor of Ireland's *Evening Press*, he was formerly editor of an English award-winning newspaper. Widely travelled, he wrote his first short story in Egypt in 1950. Since then, he has published stories, articles and plays in American, British and Irish publications. Lecturer in creative writing at a Dublin college, he has recorded some 400 broadcasts for regional B.B.C. programmes.

CONTENTS

The roly-poly figure of Brendan Behan, head tilted and his right shoulder ahead of himself as he swings along with quick bird-like spurts and a good square foot or two of hairy chest showing, is not likely to be too welcome in whatever literary heaven the ghosts of Irish writers inhabit. But Brendan is not the one who is going to be uncomfortable.

Lady Gregory will probably move away with polite distaste as he impudently quotes at her the brand of stage Irishism she created: 'My heavy blessing on you . . .' W. B. Yeats will raise a metaphysical eyebrow and wander quickly away for the restorative conversation of Madame Blavatsky. George Moore will wonder what the world of Irish literature is coming to when an object like this is produced by it.

Maybe Brian Merriman, the bawdy Irish poet of the eighteenth century, will greet him warmly and swap a few social indecencies of a kind that got the two of them banned by the Irish censor.

What about George Bernard Shaw? His vegetable bloodstream will hardly stand the raw meat of the Behan personality. John Millington Synge will scarcely swap memories of the Aran Islands, which each in their own way incorporated into their own lives. He too may be reminded that if he doesn't keep his nose clean he may get a clip of a turf-spade on the 'ridge of the skull' that will split him on 'the knob of his gullet'.

Lennox Robinson may wince with the wraith-like shudder he imported from earth as he is familiarly addressed: 'Here I am, me oul' son, a shAbbey playwright like yourself.' And then he will be reminded of the time they contributed to the same page of the *Irish Press*: 'Remember when we were diggin' the readies out of the *Irish Press* for two yards of typin' every month?'

James Joyce? It's hard to say. He will want to examine clinically a pure specimen of Dublin manhood again and slip away into some celestial johns to scribble down his reaction, or an 'epiphany' as he called it. His conscience or 'the agenbite of inwit' may be soothed a little when he hears the new arrival praise his own beloved Dublin Bay and its 'snotgreen . . . scrotumtightening sea.'

With his normal good humour Oscar Wilde may tolerate what he cannot understand. Congreve and Farquhar, Swift and Laurence Sterne will enjoy the earthy humour that is not unknown in their own uninhibited works. Congreve may sing his glorious Joan of Deptford – buxom Joan who made up her mind not 'to lie o' night alone' and was won by a sailor who:

> '. . . let fly at her
> A shot 'twixt wind and water,
> That won this fair maid's heart.'

Brendan's reply will be his lively flesh tingling rendering of 'I am Lady Chatterley's Lover' to the solemn air of 'Land of Hope and Glory'.

If things get dull in the Irish sector now and then, and the Cork author and priest, Canon Sheehan, might put his foot down once in a while, he can slip across to the French paradise – and a French paradise means wine and women – to greet Master Rusticockpiddleshankcrapwallopper himself, François Rabelais.

But no one can deny his right to be there. His passport to the Valhalla of genius is stamped with the visas of a few great works. Even those who feel uncomfortable with him will have to admit grudgingly that he was legitimately cast in the clean, hard mould of the Irish literary tradition. Oh, indeed, it was a strange and heavenly wonder that was shaped by the world of Brendan Behan.

THE BALLAD OF BRENDAN BEHAN

By Jimmy Hiney

A Springtime day, yes, one of sorrow,
A day in March – 1964
The Spotlights out, the curtain fallen,
The final bow, to his native shore.
This rebel artist, from down by Liffey,
Whose uncle gave us 'A Soldier's Song'
The grandson true, of a Fenian fighter.
Yes rebels all – in a day now gone.

At an early age he joined the Fianna,
And not – the Soldiers of Destiny,
Who still today, hold power and glory,
With a make believe of a nation free.
To serve old Ireland – the true ideals –
That was sealed in blood back in '16,
And for the truth, like others suffered,
For to Brendan Behan, 'twas no idle dream.

Afar from Ireland, her cause for freedom,
This Irish youth, got an English cell,
The Borstal boy, we know well the story,
Yes, all for Ireland, this goal of hell,
Then home deported and the specials waited
For this Irish rebel, with the determined will.
And once again Brendan Behan is prisoner,
In Mountjoy, the Curragh and Arbour Hill.

A bright spring morn, we laid him sleeping,
With a fond farewell from a soldier's pal,
And men of letters, his name saluted,
For his auld triangle, and the Royal Canal.

THE THINGS THAT BRENDAN SAID....

Soda-water: 'A good drink invented in Dublin, but better with whiskey than straight.'

The I.R.A.: 'If the big powers like America and Russia are entitled to drop big bombs, surely the I.R.A. are entitled to drop little bombs.'

Money: 'If people want me to behave like Cardinal Spellman or Billy Graham, why don't they pay me the salary those fellows are getting.'

Partition: 'Everybody in Ireland is against partition. It has me in the same camp as the Prime Minister – and I don't want to be in the same camp as the Taoiseach any more than he wants to be in the same camp as meself.'

Politicians: 'I'm not a politician. I've only got one face.'

Fame: 'Once I heard that somebody had shouted "blasphemy" at the presentation of "The Hostage" in the Olympia, I knew I was in the tradition of O'Casey and Synge.'

Religion: 'When I'm in health I'm not at all religious. But when I'm sick I'm very religious.'

Himself: 'I think I'm as well behaved as most politicians, owners of television networks, newspaper proprietors. I'm not dead and I don't belong to posterity yet. How's my health? If I felt any better I couldn't stand it.'

Prison: 'Which prison do you prefer – English or Irish?' asked an interviewer. 'English jails when you're young and Irish jails when you are older.'

Hollywood: 'To go to California and not see Hollywood is like going to Ireland and not seeing the Lakes of Killarney.'

California: 'California is the place to live. New York is the greatest city in the world, but six months a year in California is just what I want.'

Dublin: 'In Dublin you have conviviality, but no friendship. And Dublin will give you loneliness, too – but no solitude.'

Canada: 'A lot of people say I hate Canada. I don't hate any place . . . well, I make certain exceptions. Canada's the only place where I've been accused of being a Dogan. That's an Irish Catholic. I asked them for it in writing so I could show it at home.'

Toronto: 'I got a lot of dough there. It'll be a marvellous city – it's only because I've a show there I'm saying that.'

Vancouver: 'A terrible hole.'

Hamilton: 'I can't be blasphemous enough about it.'

English: 'They're like the Germans, their first cousins, a very innocent race of people. Gentle when they're taken away from their guns, their queens, their kings.'

New York: 'I think the housing for the working classes here is lousey,' he said. 'Dublin city puts you to shame. The buses are small and filthy in comparison to our buses, and the subway is a death-trap. The newspapers, too, are effin' awful.'

On the birth of his daughter, November 1963: 'This is the best thing that has happened to me since I wrote "The Quare Fellow". She's a lovely child.'

Television: Asked if he thought it was appropriate to appear drunk in front of B.B.C. television cameras. 'I thought it perfectly natural. Yes, in my case, yes.'

Ernest Hemingway and Liam O'Flaherty: 'There's plenty of violence in my writings but I am not so childishly pleased about it as they are.'
He said he was a 'very highly trained man'. He studied the drama every week from the age of 4 to 14 in 'my uncle's theatre, the old Queen's.'

The Abbey: 'In the Abbey what happens is somebody says, "Musha, will ye be putting on a pan of rashers." The Abbey actors must be the best fed crowd of players in Europe.'

The Irish: 'The Irish people were my raw material. I like some of them, the taxi-drivers, house-painters, bookies' runners. The Theatre-going people, what passes for society, I don't like and they don't like me.'

His next book: On September 3rd 1960 in an interview on Canadian Television, he talked about a new book 'The Catacombs', which he might turn into a play. 'It is about the people of Dublin. I don't write about anybody else.'

BRENDAN BEHAN—A NEW LOOK

By Sean McCann

BRENDAN BEHAN could write.
Drink
Shout
Sing
And swear.

He was a wild man, a hard man, a quare fella. He was the wildest Dublinman of the century. Everywhere you go in the city on the Liffey you will hear stories about him. He was a roaring legend during his life. He is not long dead and the cult of Behanism is rampant.

In the places where he used to go (and from the stories there were few places he didn't go and do something extraordinary) they will never forget him.

'If there were only three Irishmen left in the world you'd find two of them in a corner talking about the other. We're always backbiting. But if the third man happened to be Brendan he'd be away in his corner singing, writing, shouting and swearing at the other two.'

That was the sort of man Brendan Behan was. Physically he was a brooding man; a black cloud of a man. He deteriorated very quickly from a brawny, curly black haired, pleasant individual to a scarlet faced, bloodshot eyed, tousled haired, badly dressed man in a few short years. But whatever he may have lost physically he made up for it in the way he used words, in the way he could write, sing, shout and swear.

In this book new, and even startling, facets of the man Behan are revealed for the first time. The Behan known to old lags and famous writers; the domesticated Brendan and his wife, whose only serious complaint about him was that he was always late for meals; the comment of the Governor of Mountjoy Prison that Brendan was the second untidiest prisoner he had ever known. These recollections make this the most complete portrait of the man as a writer, rebel and drinker ever attempted. However before the detailed examination it is worth looking at the life of Behan as a whole.

There is a rumour that he was born on February 9, 1923, but it is likely to remain a rumour. The most patient and prolonged research by officials in Ireland's Registry of Births, Marriages and Deaths has failed to produce one iota of evidence that Brendan was even born at all. Officially he just happened . . . a miraculous accident or oversight and a reasonable good start for a man like himself. To my constant requests for a copy of Brendan's birth certificate I received the following official reply.

Uimh 5/8/645.H2
Oifig an Ard-Chlaraitheora,
Teach an Chustaim,
Dublin 1.
10–8–65.

A Chara,

In reply to your application of the 5th inst. I have to acquaint you that search has been made for the entry of the birth of Brendan Behan from the year 1920 to 1925 inclusive but no entry has been found in the records for the period stated corresponding with the particulars given by you.

Mise le meas,
P.O. Cinneide,
Ard-Chlaraitheoir.

According to the family version he saw the light of day in Holles Street Hospital – on the hated south side of the city. The real Dublinman's Hospital is the Rotunda, on the North side, and to be born there is the mark of every true Dubliner. But although his family lived near the Rotunda, for some reason – either a little bit of shooting in the vicinity or a high birth rate on that day – Brendan, as yet unborn, was taken across the city to Holles Street.

Anytime afterwards if you wanted to annoy Brendan you only had to mention this accident of birth. The question of birth came up on the first occasion I ever met him. He was in that in-between state of drunkenness and sobriety. 'Are you from Dublin?' he bellowed and the bar patrons looked up expectantly. Before he got an answer he bellowed on. 'You don't (effin') well sound like it. Come back when you're born in Dublin.'

It was fun then to taunt him with being a native of the snob south side of the city. And to taunt him further by letting him know that I had been born in the Rotunda. 'Touché,' he muttered and lapsed into silence and 'a pint of gargle.'

He often told a story about his birth – for even full of beer he could keep his head and always knew the value of a good story. That's why so many stories are repeated so often in so many different places with so essentially different facts. He was being defended on a charge of entering England illegally. His solicitor apologised for his behaviour and put it down to him being a

'love child of the Irish revolution'. 'The mother was scandalised, never mind slandered,' he'd tell and grin a toothless grin at the memory.

As a child he realised that he was a 'bit of a hard chaw'. He said that his mother said there was so much divilment in him that he would 'hang a parish'. His father said that he 'didn't know where he got me – and me only a high infant in William Street'.

It was the French Sisters of Charity who first took him into school, a small red brick house with castor oil plants in the window, in a claustrophobic part of Dublin by the side of the Canal. He loved it there. 'I was their little pet,' he said. Then he passed to the Christian Brothers. 'I hated them and they hated me.' They parted by mutual consent when Brendan was 13. It was Borstal in England and prison after prison that gave him his real education.

There was Dublin's Mountjoy Jail, Strangeways in Manchester, The Glasshouse in the Curragh. From these experiences came 'The Quare Fellow', 'The Hostage', 'Borstal Boy', 'The Scarperer'.

Brendan was a lot of things before he became a writer. Most famous perhaps was his house painting. 'A bloody dirty and dangerous job', he said. He never said the same about carrying bombs or rifles or shooting at policemen. Or about his years in prison. But he wrote about these things. Not about house painting.

Whatever was revolutionary in him had long roots. He came from a long line of rebels who were nurtured over a tenement fire. A grandmother of his was jailed for illegal possession of explosives at the age of seventy. A grandfather was one of The Invincibles (they murdered Lord Cavendish on a Sunday morning in Phoenix Park in 1882); both his parents fought in the War of Independence and in The Troubles; his father was interned with Sean T. O'Kelly, later president of Ireland; his uncle Peadar Kearney wrote the Irish National Anthem, *The Soldier's Song*. Brendan was only 9 when he joined the Fianna, the junior movement of the I.R.A. By the time he was 16 he was carrying messages for the Chief of Staff of the I.R.A. Sean Russell (he died in a German submarine in the last war).

It was in Liverpool that Brendan was caught following in his Granny's footsteps – she had been sentenced only a short time before – carrying explosives. For this he went to Borstal for 18 months – time, as it turned out, that couldn't have been better spent. From it came 'Borstal Boy'.

He went back to the I.R.A. – and was caught again. This time it was 14 years for shooting at a policeman. He only served four. 'The sister of the man who sentenced me gave me a coffee pot for a wedding present a few years after.'

He would never agree that he was a wild man. 'I'm not a war-like man – as a matter of fact a highly ineffectual one. The I.R.A. had sufficient good military sense never to make me more than a messenger boy.'

He was an expert with explosives and had a few words to say about bombs. 'Why are the Irish or even a section of the Irish the only ones not permitted to use bombs?' he asked. 'Is it because we only use little ones and the others use big ones?'

Nevertheless bombs, little ones ('I carried gelignite, dynamite isn't safe') got him into trouble and it wasn't until 1946 when a general amnesty was granted to all political prisoners that Behan was free again. Back he went to England where he was again thrown into jail – this time for helping Irish revolutionaries escape from the police.

On this occasion an I.R.A. man was to be 'rescued' from Leyhill prison in Surrey and it was Brendan's job after the rescue to guard a Park Ranger in the vicinity of the prison. 'A decent man. A quiet respectable Irishman who, even though he was employed by the British Imperial Majesty, never spoke a word against us or his parent country. Helpful, not a bit of trouble. And the only effin' thing I did to convince him of our good intentions was to hold a 45 revolver at his head all the time. Cocked.' The 'rescue' was a success. This was probably his most successful 'rebel' encounter and he acknowledged his ineffectualness when he called himself 'the most captured soldier in Irish history'.

Paris came next. Bits of writing ('mostly dirty stories'). Bits of house painting and one or two stints as a sailor. He treated a visit to France like an excursion to Bray and he would slip over on one of the fishing trawlers that came into Dublin. Then under cover of darkness – he had no passport at this time – he would slip on to French soil for an evening out. On one occasion he was missing from his normal Dublin haunts for a long time. 'Then one day', says a close friend, 'I saw him rolling along, fit and sun burned, a little leather bag in his hand. I was up a ladder painting and when Brendan saw me he roared out. "Come down outa that. I've strange tales to tell of foreign parts." He had been an official member of a crew that had been to Spain and back.'

Not only had he strange tales of foreign parts but the Irish theatre managements thought his tales of Irish parts were a bit strange too. Especially 'The Quare Fellow' which was rejected by just about every theatre management in Dublin until it was staged in the small unsubsidised Pike Theatre. Instant success was born then.

Brendan took to writing a weekly column for the Irish Press in 1954. There was a smattering of real Dublin and real Behan in it. While he was with the paper he made a lot of friends. His greatest was M. J. MacManus. When MacManus, who was literary editor, died, Brendan walked three miles to the funeral and back again on a wet dismal day. His shoes were leaking. He hadn't the price of the bus ride, never mind the price of a new pair of shoes.

That was one of his troubles. Money came and went like the tide. He was an easy touch, as they say in Dublin. If you wanted money you would get it from Brendan – if he had it. If he borrowed from you you would always get it back.

'What year did you stop writing your newspaper column, Brendan?' 'How the effin' hell would I know the date. Dates is only for the police.'

On another occasion he said: 'I stopped writing for De Valera's Irish Press the day before I became effin' well famous. And that was the day when I could afford at long last to pay for me effin' gargle.'

It was the production of 'The Quare Fellow' by Joan Littlewood in London that really brought him fame. The play was a universal success. And wherever it went Brendan went too. And with him his voice. Interjections in the auditoriums, brawling in the pubs, inarticulate appearances on television. Brendan, the papers said, was the original drunken Paddy.

Ed Murrow had a name for him. He called him 'difficulties beyond our control' when he had to cut Behan out of a three-way Small World discussion. Jackie Gleason, who was in the same show, said: 'Behan came over 100 proof. It wasn't an act of God but an act of Guinness.' *The Daily News* said: 'If the celebrated playwright wasn't pickled he gave the best imitation of rambling alcoholism you ever saw.'

Even the B.B.C. wasn't immune to Behanism. Their switchboard was jammed with calls after Brendan appeared on the ultra-respectable Panorama programme. Behan was surprised at the reaction. 'Yes I had a few drinks. Everyone in Ireland knows that I take a drink and takes no notice. In Dublin the whole thing would have passed without comment.'

But Dublin was sitting up and taking notice. The appearance on TV was the subject of much critical controversy in Ireland. A one time Lord Mayor of Dublin ascribed Brendan's popularity to the fact that he was 'the living specimen of the type of people many writers want to describe us (The Irish) as'.

On the other side a Dail deputy said: 'Don't abandon Behan because he is a bit hard to handle. If he were the really solid type he wouldn't write anything.' Irish newspapers joined in the battle. 'A false image of Ireland' 'He's playing the stage Irishman' 'He does it for publicity – and money' 'A disgrace to Ireland'. And Brendan retorted: 'They're just bloody jealous.' And he left it at that.

The *Irish Times* in its portrait gallery summed up the Behan situation. 'There are persons of bourgeois respectability in the city of Dublin who nourish a secret unease. It is that one day they may be proceeding on their middleclass way, chatting smoothly with their employer or their bank manager when suddenly across the street will come a loud and ebullient 'View-halloo' followed by a colourful and uninhibited commentary on things in general. It will, of course, be Mr. Brendan Behan, who enjoys carrying on conversations with the width of the street between himself and his interlocuter. Mr. Behan has the voice for it but few of his friends have the nerve. Still, it is one of the occupational risks involved in knowing Mr. Behan, and all who know him have decided that it is worth it.'

Nothing could have summed up reaction to Behan more effectively than that one paragraph . . . although it was not really true that everyone decided that it was worth it. One well known columnist, talking quietly to a friend in fashionable Grafton

Street one day, was hailed by Brendan from the other sidewalk. 'How's the writing going? That oul column of yours is only retail business. Why don't you get into the wholesale trade like me? Books . . . plays . . . money.'

And Brendan was gone. But not all his cross street jibes were so innocent. His extreme vulgarity was often aroused by gentility. Seated one snowy, cold day on the sea wall of the Liffey he saw passing on the other side of the broad quay a well known nature writer. 'Hey missus', he roared like an articulate polar bear, 'how's the Blue Tits?'

Few miss Brendan as much as newspaper editors. He was always good for a diversion – and a headline. Wherever he went there were newspapermen in too – and they were usually rewarded. Like the night in Wyndham's Theatre in London where 'The Hostage' was playing. Behan rumpled, crumpled and very thirsty panicked the cast and audience when he burst into the theatre. He strode into the foyer, banged at the box office and demanded tickets for himself and a friend. Before taking his seat he went outside and entertained the queue waiting to get into the theatre with a selection of Irish songs. Then he took up a collection for a busker whose raincoat and hat he had borrowed. Afterwards he said 'I thought it a perfectly natural thing to do. I've been a busker myself . . . not a very successful one. I'm not by any means an exhibitionist . . .'

After the busking he charged into the theatre and as the audience stood to cheer him he roared 'eejits'. He sat down – temporarily – then jumped to his feet, faced the audience from his front row seat and roared: 'Up the rebels, up the Chinese'. All through the play he interrupted the actors. At one stage an actor who was playing an I.R.A. man shouted back at him: 'I'll have you shot'. Behan's reply was impossible to print. When 'God Save the Queen' was played Brendan roared again: 'Up the Irish'.

He lived a life that was never a middlecourse. It was extremes or nothing, life or death, whiskey or water. But water was only for swimming in. He was a great man for 'going in for a dip'. Even on the coldest days he would plunge in like a big sea lion. He would stay in the water until he was blue with the cold. He learned to swim in the canal near his home. His ancestors had been reared on its banks. One aunt who lived in a house by a lock, would invite all and sundry to 'drop in anytime you're passing'. Brendan took it literally once and was almost drowned. Afterwards he became a good swimmer. And he wasn't always worried about the convention of dressing. Once on a crowded beach he ran to the water with not a stitch on roaring as he went: 'Close your eyes, girls, I'm coming through'.

That was how he liked his drink too – naked. But the legend of Behan the drinker needs a closer look. He studied the art of drinking under the experienced and critical eye of his Granny English. He graduated easily from the glass of cordial, given free to the children of the customers of Dublin's public houses, to the black, robust nourishment of Guinness. As a student drinker he made the acquaintance of almost every 'grocer's curate' – as Irish barmen were called – and in this way laid the foundations of the exaggerated legends. To listen to some people you would imagine that Brendan drank not just in pint glasses but in barrels, hogheads and swam in a sea of poteen and porter. The cold sober assessment of a professional barman has classified him as a five-pint man. Even this was in his early days and after that he was drunk. In his last decade almost one brandy was enough to make his day drunken.

When he was writing he tried not to drink. 'Chastity and water is the only formula for writing.' That's why his output was so small. 'As regards the drink', he said, 'I can only say that when I was growing up drunkenness was not regarded as a social disgrace. To get enough to eat was regarded as an achievement. To get drunk was a victory.'

At this rate he won many a victory in life. And the newspaper cuttings are there to prove it. Flick through a bundle. 'Behan arrested in London' 'Behan fined in Toronto' 'It's a lie I'm not dead' 'He wasn't dead – only drunk' 'Behan banned in New York' 'London spree cost Behan £150'.

After the spree in London he appeared in a Bow Street Court sporting a black eye and a cut cheek. He was dressed in a crumpled green suit, brown sandals and a white shirt borrowed from his agent. Asked if he had anything to say Behan replied: 'I was given 14 years for shooting at the coppers but this eye didn't come from the cops. They were very kind and very civil.' After paying a small fine he slipped out through a side door and headed for a pub where he had two whiskeys and three bottles of stout. Stout was the only drink he found good enough to follow the whiskey. 'Whiskey is too good to be sullied with water.'

He liked to talk about the drink almost as much as he liked to drink it. And he often pretended to have more taken than he really had. He would lapse into long dumb periods and then lift a wildly tousled head from a bar counter and shatter the drinkers with a mouthful of well chosen words that left nothing to the imagination. He liked to play up to the legend of the

22

drinker. 'Drink is good enough any time of the day. I take it for breakfast, dinner and tea. No that's a lie . . . I take a cuppa tea and a rasher sometimes but that's only to cod the wife.'

If he wasn't talking about the drink on his pub crawls he'd be singing songs that he made up himself. He had a great voice for singing ballads – like a foghorn that had gone wrong and could not be fixed. Some of the songs he wrote – like 'The Ould Triangle' are already part of the folk music of Ireland. Others were songs for the moment only. When 'Borstal Boy' was banned in Ireland (it still is) he was hurt – but he tried to laugh at it. He made up his own words to the tune of MacNamara's Band.

> *Oh, me name is Brendan Behan, I'm the latest of the banned,*
> *Although we're small in numbers we're the best banned in the land,*
> *We're read at wakes and weddin's and in every parish hall,*
> *And under library counters sure you'll have no trouble at all.*

At the end of the song he would bellow: 'I've banned the Censorship Board and there's no appeal from my decision'.

He said he didn't give a damn whether they banned his books or not. 'The Irish aren't my audience . . . they're my raw material. I immortalise them. The people I care about in Ireland: the taxi drivers, house painters, bookies' runners, they don't buy books very much and they don't live by books or literature except newspapers with the racing results.' But for all his joking he was badly hurt by the banning of 'Borstal Boy' and by the delay in recognising his playwriting ability. Above all else he wanted recognition in his own country.

He took up writing, he said, because it was easier than house painting. He wrote his first piece – a letter to a paper – when he was 13. Poetry in Irish, short stories, essays, plays and books followed.

Once he was arguing with 'a person who writes plays and has another occupation . . . he's an ex officer of the law . . . a legal person in Ireland. He says to me "My plays will be remembered long after you are dead and rotten". Well, I said, I want to tell you something and that is this. First of all I'm not interested in having my plays remembered after I'm dead and rotten. Second I don't particularly like the thought of being dead and rotten.'

He would poke fun at anyone. But there was another side to him. If he didn't like a person – and he could hate you as quickly as he could like you – he made it as uncomfortable as possible for them. In a pub in the centre of the city a famous Dublin businessman joined in the chorus of people asking Brendan to sing. 'Ah, go on Brendan, give us a song. Sing Brendan,' shouted

23

the notable. And a hush came over the room. This man's call was usually answered. Brendan lifted his bleary head and looked the man in the face. 'Who the . . . hell are you?' He knew well enough who the man was. Afterwards he said: 'Why the . . . hell should I sing for him. He was never introduced to me.'

His bad language worried him sometimes. 'I know it's bad but how the effin' hell can I write the way Irishmen talk if I don't use the effin' word. After all that effer Lawrence got away with it. It's a word that's part of our international heritage.'

He always made sure the word didn't enter conversation when there were children about. But he didn't differentiate between men and women. What was good enough for one was good enough for all.

The trouble with painting a picture of Brendan is that 'The word' causes a lot of trouble. Without it his conversation doesn't ring true. And a blank doesn't convey the real meaning at all. Certainly it got him into a lot of trouble in life. But then life found Brendan a fair lot of trouble. The best thing he ever did, he said, was to get married. His widow – he always referred in conversation to 'her' or 'she' or 'the first wife' – is Beatrice, the daughter of an artist, an artist herself and a gentle person. When they were together Brendan was a different person. The best portrait of them comes from the *Irish Press*.

'The Behans never come down town. They make a royal progress. Brendan, the curls low on his forehead, like a cheerful Julius Caesar bestowing the accolade of friendship on innumerable acquaintances. Beatrice, slender, like a gentle nun . . .'

After their wedding they lived in a couple of houses before moving to the unlikeliest place of all for Brendan. The Embassy covered district of Ballsbridge, the most exclusive suburb in Dublin. There they took up residence behind a dull red door with no bell or knocker and the word 'Cuig' (Irish for five) on the gate.

'How did I get here,' Brendan growled at me once. 'I paid for the effin' place to give it a tone of respectability.'

The best thing that ever happened to him happened here. A daughter was born to Beatrice and Brendan just a few months before he died.

His story will probably recall that he died from the drink . . . his death certificate provides the complete answer. On March 20th, 1964, at the Meath Hospital. Brendan Behan, 5, Anglesea Road, Ballsbridge. Male. Married. 41 years. Writer. Cause of death: Hepatic coma, Fatty degeneration of liver. Signed Peter Sheridan, Occupier, Meath Hospital.

24

PART ONE

In the beginning...

... was the seed and the planting ... the street, the open doors, the rebel songs sung around tenement fires, the dying embers of a civil war. In the beginning too was the searing inspiration of Borstal ... a gun battle ... prison ... the first poem and the shaping of the writer that was to be Brendan Behan. His first book ... his first play and, as he used to call her, 'my first wife'. This was the beginning ...

Russell Street

1

GROWING UP

By Anthony Butler

IT is impossible to understand Brendan Behan without understanding the city that made him. Dublin was half the man and all his life. Its people, its places, its politics and its way of living provided the anvil on which the man was beaten to outsize manhood.

But the Dublin into which he was born has almost vanished and survives only in small pockets. Russell Street still has its huge brewery and its laundry while a new seedman's premises gives it a touch of colour. The house belonging to Mrs. English, Brendan Behan's grandmother, no longer stands and its neighbours are gone also. Number fourteen; tall and with a brick frontage – it was there he spent his boyhood sharing the back parlour and the front basement with the rest of his family.

Today there are few residents in Russell Street and the memory of the Behans is faint.

'A quiet family; leastwise I never heard much about them . . .'

'I remember the time Brendan fell into the canal. Drownin' he was. An' I ran into the Behans . . . an what d'yeh think was said . . . What d'yeh think? "Is that so?" cum the answer, "is that so? Ah sure Providence will protect him . . ." and not a move to see how he was . . .'

'The Granny English owned four other houses . . . comfortably off the Behans were . . . comfortable-like' . . .

It has been said that Russell Street was made up of tenements but this is over-descriptive. Certainly it was no slum.

Over the bridge which jumped the railway and the canal below was Jones Road known from one end of Ireland to the other for here the All-Ireland competitions of the Gaelic Athletic Association were played each year. When the finals of the hurling and football competitions were played they came from the four corners of the country. Big brawny men with faces scrubbed sharp with wind and polished with rain. Great belted coats and huge peaked caps.

'Go to an All-Ireland Final. Are yeh mad? Mix up with an effin' bunch of Culchies? Bogmen! Enough turf to do for the year if yeh got the scrapin's of the boots.'

Russell Street wasn't interested in Gaelic games and gave all its devotion to soccer. It wasn't a wealthy place and there was a good deal of poverty. Ironically the houses had once belonged to the wealthy. The struggle with want and hunger was sometimes fought out under graceful plaster ceilings decorated with scrolled plasterwork that came from the hands of Italian craftsmen. Miserable fires were lit in grates surrounded by massive and elegant mantelpieces.

Drink and laughter were the weapons they used to beat off despair and the fight was seldom lost. They were reinforced by the close intimacy in which they spent their over-crowded lives and this gave the strength of the tribe to Russell Street. The doors of the houses were often open and the shuttling of the inhabitants wove the tight and real fabric of a genuine community. There was concern and communication; there was a full and significant existence.

Jones Road over the bridge was also a challenge and there were constant urges to respectability. Great white cascades of net curtains often fell into place on the windows, held by wide bands of brass and framing a stuffed bird or animal. Furniture was not a great problem and the hurried departure of the British in 1922 flooded the second-hand market with mahogany sideboards and other massive articles.

Down the street in the winter came the ass and carts selling fuel by the stone and this would often be in the form of coalblocks. The bell-men with their great drays and bags of coal rarely sounded their sales message in Russell Street as they passed on to more prosperous areas. Summer was the Italian and his gaily painted hand cart and his shrill bugle announcing thick custard-like ice-cream. The scrapmen came too pushing deep wooden prams and giving away balloons and gilt-covered lead soldiers for jam jars and bottles.

The streets were almost all illuminated by soft gaslight caged in glass boxes with sloping sides and lit each night by a man who came around with a flame on the end of a long pole. In the homes themselves gas was used and oil lamps were also common.

Trams provided most of the public transport in Dublin; great glass palaces that swayed backward and forward with agonised creaks until it seemed they must disintegrate. On the older models the upper deck was open to the wind and rain and the passengers sat on wooden-ribbed seats listening to the music of the loud sparking hiss of the trolley against the overhead wires. The driver was a real commander who stood upright and vigilant like a man at the bridge of a ship. There was dignity and a sense of great skill in the way he spun the huge brass-knobbed controls.

When Brendan was young, horse traffic predominated and he often wandered amongst the hackney cabs and the sidecars that plied for hire in the main streets. The sidecar is perhaps better known as the Irish jaunting car – a vehicle with huge wheels and two benches running in line with the shafts. A journey on one of these was like travelling on a mobile and slightly drunken Matterhorn.

A rich and creative language was still spoken by most of the people in the city and Brendan learned his lesson in a good school. The phrases and images of everyday conversation were strong and vivid.

'Your blood's worth bottlin' '

'He'd drink porter out of a polisman's boot . . .'

'Gimme a pint of stout and a bottle be the neck . . .'

If one citizen made a solemn and obscene recommendation to another it would usually be met by the dignified reply: 'An' yer sister!'

The theatre was another Dublin influence that fed his mind. He regularly attended the Queen's Theatre which at that time was the poor man's Abbey. Its repertoire consisted of melodramas, many of them patriotic, and its presentations were calculated to squeeze the heart like an emotional lemon. Nothing was spared to create effect and I remember the awe with which I watched a real live horse going in through the stage door for a performance of 'My Old Kentucky Home'.

Clothing a family in those days could be effected cheaply from the open-air stalls of Cole's Lane. Off O'Connell Street this huddle of wooden huts, knit together by narrow lanes paved with huge slabs, was a colourful and useful market for the poor. Well-stocked with second-hand clothes, shoes and household necessities it solved many problems.

'Are yeh buyin' Ma'am. Ah, buy a gansey for the young fella. Lovely. Chape.'

The old-world courtesy with which the customer was greeted would often change rapidly to tougher language if some boy interfered with the goods on the stall.

'Eff off you and go home to your Oul' wan. Go on. Eff off.'

To which there was only one possible answer worthy of the insulted one's dignity: 'An' yer sister!'

But although the city was still Victorian in its appearance and habits there was a vast alteration in its outlook from the days when it was subject to the British crown. A rebellion in 1916; savage guerrilla warfare against the British Army between 1918

29

and 1921 followed by a Civil War, had established a Government of Irishmen in Dublin.

The bitterness generated in the Civil War poisoned individual and political relationships and the extreme Republicans could not accept the fact of membership of the British Commonwealth. Indeed, for them, the revolutionary Republic had never been disestablished and they looked on the existing state as an usurper of authority – a green cloak for the reality of imperialism. It was something to be destroyed.

The Behan family belonged to the Republican camp and even though a marching song written by their uncle was adopted as the National Anthem it did not convert them to the ruling party. It was inevitable that Brendan should adopt the political beliefs of his family, particularly the uncompromising and fierce ideals of his mother tinged as they were with the red hue of socialism.

As he grew up the newspapers carried regular reports of shootings, explosions and disturbance. Whenever he went through O'Connell Street he could see the pitted marks of bullets on the General Post Office and on Nelson's Pillar.

Some time around the early thirties he joined Fianna Eireann, the Republican Boy Scouts and donned their military-style green jacket with round brass buttons in two rows down the chest topped by a dashing slouch hat. Although it took members on hikes and fed them on legends of Ireland it had the more serious purpose of preparing them for service in the Republican Army. Brendan was now in direct contact with another Dublin – Republican Dublin, with its fierce and consuming flame of sacrifice and idealism.

Irish Republicanism is an extraordinary phenomenon and it represents romantic patriotism in its purest and most intense form. Those who serve it become for a time immune to the needs and desires of everyday life. An ecstasy of this kind can rarely last for very long and it is true to say that a generation of Republicans is not more than four years in most cases. Nonetheless it leaves an immutable stamp on the souls of those who are touched by it.

To the highly sensitive Brendan it made a deep appeal and he read widely and earnestly as well as taking part in all the activities of the Fianna. It also stimulated his literary talents and he was, at an early age, a regular contributor of poems and stories to the organisation's magazine.

In 1932 the city was reaching a high point of history and excitement as the General Election approached. The Fianna Fail party led by Mr. De Valera represented in the Dail a slightly modified form of extreme Republicanism and it enjoyed the tacit support of the I.R.A. The party gave an assent to the Government which was less than total and it was their policy to reverse the formal loyalty given to the British Crown under the Constitution of the day.

It was a fierce campaign and living close to the centre of Dublin it was easy for Brendan, small and fat and young, to be engulfed by the whirlpool of passion and curiosity which spun nightly in the streets. Meetings were broken up and although not an official 'job' the I.R.A. helped to disorganise the Government's campaign. There was hope and uneasiness; expectation and fear. I can still vividly recall the heart-stopping experience of the monstrous public meetings which took place in College Green.

When the then Mr. De Valera spoke the street would be packed with incredible masses of people and the electric atmosphere which prevailed is unknown today. The vast crowd seemed to have one will and one energy. When the cheering rose it appeared to be more than the sum of individual efforts and every swaying movement was an emotional unitary response.

Fianna Fail won and there was a surge of tremendous optimism throughout the country which negated for a time the shadow of the world depression which had begun to make itself felt. The Millennium was at hand or so it seemed to Republicans.

In the first years the young and vigorous Fianna Fail administration tackled the nation's problems with drive and enthusiasm but it was impossible to deliver the political demands of the I.R.A. No one could.

It was still a very large and well-armed military group, having inherited the revolutionary arsenals of the past. Its leaders exercised considerable power and from any point of view found it difficult to relinquish their unique position.

By this time, Brendan was on the fringe of I.R.A. activity; he was learning about the jobs that had to be done – the blowing up of a statue; the burning of a British Legion Hall; the wrecking of a shop which unwisely displayed the Union Jack. He would hear echoes of plans for assassinations or executions as they were called.

In addition there were the innumerable processions to cemeteries to commemorate the memory of those who died for Ireland. Brendan acquired a remarkable knowledge of all those buried in the city. One example is to be found in 'Borstal Boy'.

Towards the end of the book when he describes with nostalgic detail the landscape of Dublin as, returning from imprisonment in England, he sees it from the deck of the ship, he mentions a

Tricolour away in the distance flying over the grave of Dan Head in Kilbarrack Cemetery. Dan Head was a member of the I.R.A. who was killed in the attack on the Customs House during the war of Independence. I checked Brendan's statement with a brother of Volunteer Head who confirmed that it was correct.

Mr. Head's father erected a flagpole beside the grave of his son and for many years on the anniversary of the shooting he put a new Tricolour on the mast.

Intoxication and expectation – of what no one seemed quite sure – were the keynotes of Republican Dublin in 1934 and '35. Riots were quite common and for Brendan it was often cheaper and more exciting than the pictures to skirt some conflict with the police and join in a vast scamper before a baton charge.

Armistice Day on November the 11th always gave rise to trouble. Poppy-snatching was a light-hearted sport which was widely practised. The emblems would be torn from the coats of stout and respectable citizens while large stones would go through the windows of shops displaying them. The parade of Irishmen who served with the British forces in France also led to some violence.

Easter parades to Glasnevin Cemetery were other occasions when disturbances arose. To add fuel to an already explosive fire, members of the Communist Party of Ireland – all twenty-eight of them – would fall in uninvited behind the I.R.A. ranks and display conspicuous red rosettes in their buttonholes. This rearguard was understandably subject to angry attacks by citizens gathered along the route.

On a memorable occasion only one member of the Red group reached the cemetery, the remainder having been detained to discuss their views with sundry groups through the medium of sticks and iron-shod boots.

The Spanish Civil War which started in 1936 disturbed the I.R.A. Some were for the Spanish Republicans because they were Republicans and others supported the Madrid Government for ideological reasons. Because Nazi Germany gave help to Franco, and Hitler was an enemy of Britain, another section was in favour of the anti-reds. This split was to wreck the I.R.A. organisation until it pulled itself together in 1938 under the austere and dedicated leadership of Sean Russell.

One tortured soul of that period admitted that while he openly supported the Spanish Government he secretly prayed for Franco. A consequence of Republican inertia was the development of independent actions by Republican supporters.

Brendan took part in several minor jobs of this kind and was not unknown to the political debates and conspiracies which centred on the monument of Horatio Nelson in O'Connell Street. Every day a dozen conspiracies and 'jobs' were discussed with easy abandon. Although the police had easy access to the plans they were hampered by the fact that they never knew which one was likely to be implemented.

Brendan Behan and his family were affected by the big building strike of 1937 and there was much unofficial I.R.A. activity in connection with this. One plan called for the seizure of the Mansion House and in a mood of generosity a friend of mine asked me to take part. I more or less agreed but pointed out that my mother expected me home at ten o'clock each night so that I could only participate in rebellion on a shift basis.

The Behans were supporters of the Spanish Government and this was due in the main to the convictions of Kathleen Behan, Brendan's mother. Her son Brian has described her as wolflike in her intensity. Some time ago I heard her sing the 'Red Flag' at a reception by Claddagh Records to mark the launching of a new record of Irish traditional music. It was something.

Although no longer young she tipped the words and music with fire. With a glass of brandy held aloft and defiance in every swing of her wrist and half-sway of her body she conjured an image of barricades and revolt:

> *Then by this banner swear we all,*
> *To bear it forward 'til we fall*
> *For dungeons dark or gallows drear*
> *This song will be our parting hymn*
> *Then raise the scarlet banner high*
> *Within its folds we'll live or die*
> *Let cowards mock or traitors sneer*
> *We'll keep the Red Flag flying here.*

In 1937, however, a domestic upheaval turned the minds of the Behans from politics for a brief moment. The vast efforts of the Fianna Fail Government to solve the housing problem caught them in its mesh and they were given accommodation in the working-class housing scheme in Kimmage.

They were not particularly grateful for the opportunity to obtain a modern home and approached their departure with the happy anticipation of a Ukrainian peasant leaving for Omsk. Their complaints were somewhat justified as the municipal authorities charged with the administration of housing plans showed little imagination. They broke up old tenement communities; integrated and meaningful. Concentrated within small

33

areas these had their own patterns of tradition and custom, and no family was isolated in the web of human relations and sympathy which they spun. This could make some of the worst privations endurable.

The removal of the Behans to Kimmage disrupted their way of life and their sense of belonging. They were more unfortunate than most as their intellectualism and political philosophies cut them off from their new neighbours. They were not absorbed in the group.

People in the Kildare Road area of Kimmage where the Behan family resided are reluctant to speak of their early life in the area. Some will obviously and platitudinously flatter Brendan's memory but the majority have little to say or are outspoken in their hostility. The latter individuals are infrequent. It is certain that the Behans still found their intimate friends and interests outside Kimmage.

In any event these City Corporation developments or the 'schemes' as they were called developed a ghetto-like mentality amongst the inhabitants. They were separated from the rest of society by the simple fact of their address; they became music hall jokes and sly stories circulated that they kept coal in the baths and used toilet seats to frame pictures of national heroes. It was understandable that many of them were aggressive towards other social strata.

Nevertheless the move to Kimmage widened Brendan's horizons and charged his sensibility with fresh experience. If it was only a visit to their local pawnshop they were brought in contact with the Jewish district around Clanbrasil Street. At that time the Jews were richer in human qualities than anything else. They moulded their area into a corner of Eastern Europe with overtones of the Middle Fast. The long beards, the flood of Yiddish, the quick gestures, the bright intensity were always impressive and curious.

Dublin affected Brendan in another way because of the change. It shattered the last shell of localisation that inhibited him somewhat in Russell Street and opened his mind and senses to the wide range of the city's loveliness. From the upper windows of 70, Kildare Road he could look across the city; across the bay, to the Hill of Howth and before development extended he had an uninterrupted view of the Dublin Mountains.

It is something to indicate the aspects of Dublin that played their part in the life of Brendan Behan, but any such account would be incomplete without some reference to the inimitable and intangible quality of the city as a whole.

It is one of the world's most extraordinary places and anyone who spends more than three months there will hate leaving and will always be haunted to return. No one has ever defined its charm and its secret, but this is largely because there is no single element that can be isolated. It is a total effect built up of a thousand influences.

James Joyce was crucified on its memory all the days of his exile, and Shaw who lived there for only a brief period admitted it had shaped his psyche beyond alteration. Brendan Behan was steeped in its mystique, and he pulsed with the ancient rhythms of its being. Perhaps something of the peculiar quality of Dublin is to be found in its physical features. At least they give some idea of what it does to its inhabitants and most of these have never availed of all it can offer.

It is a comfortable place to live in and it doesn't overwhelm its people or its visitors by vastness or splendour. The River Liffey for instance runs its watery avenue in a straight line through the city's centre, and at no point is it wider than a docker's spit. When there is a particularly low tide, it is almost drained to emptiness revealing homely mud flats sprinkled with the discarded belongings of the citizens, old prams, bicycles, and on one classical occasion – a grand piano.

It has no architectural highlights but there is a personality in its design and environment that invades every inch of its being. It manages by an intimate magic to give a village atmosphere for its 700,000 inhabitants. Its narrow-spaced grid of churches comfort by sight or sound in every area, and an equally close mesh of public houses holds in comfort the gregarious pleasures of its easy citizens.

Set on the shores of a neat bay, it is surrounded by small mountains of many shapes – long-curved ranges or sharp volcano-peaked hills. Within the jurisdiction of the Dublin City Council you can stand above lonely cliffs dropping sheer into the sea and dotted with the nests of sea birds; you can walk along deserted paths amongst fields of grazing cattle or watch herds of deer in natural surroundings drifting like brown clouds over vast parklands.

Wandering out beside its deserted canals you can find great forests of reed, six feet in height and unpeopled tow paths that lead past stretches of water and locks that recall, in their tranquil settings, the paintings of Constable or the poems of John Clare.

Within six miles of the city you can find yourself on deserted moorland amid great bogs, where mountain roads wander thin and desolate through landscapes identical with the Scottish

Highlands. Within the same range you can find a dozen isolated lakes. If you want an English countryside, lush and cultivated you need only travel out the road to the old public house 'The Wren's Nest' where Brendan drank and helped to maintain the five-hundred-year tradition of the inn. Here too the Liffey flows broad, shallow and sluggish towards the sea.

If you want a total isolation within sight and sound of the city's centre you can wander over the hundreds of acres of flats at low tide along five miles of the coast. Here hundreds of sea birds sit on the sand and a shout will send a vast umbrella of whirring wings into the sky.

Weather too, is an important feature in the life of Dublin. The climate is temperate and you'll never freeze to death or perish from sunstroke, yet the city gets a sample of everything. There will be weeks in the summer when they'll lie and bake on the broad strands of Malahide or Killiney, and in winter it will be unusual if snow doesn't stay for fifteen or sixteen days in the hills to give a taste of winter sports.

You can find as much elsewhere; the United States or New Zealand has as much to offer but you'll have to travel hundreds of miles to get it. The wonder and miracle of Dublin is its compactness. Within a radius of eight miles a man can have every experience he would ever wish to enjoy. It is complete in itself. Indeed it could be said that Dublin is not a city; it is a lazy man's continent.

It is necessary to stress all this if we are to find a real clue to the mind of Brendan Behan or any other Dublin writer for that matter. Their exposure to Dublin gives them a developed sensibility that few others ever attain. It gives completeness.

The Dublin of Brendan Behan is a fine place but if ever one individual symbolised it, he was that symbol. Kind, outrageous, sophisticated, naive, talented . . . he matched in his psychological landscape the varied features of her face. Now he is part of its history and treasure. Now he is at one with it.

2

HIS PARENTS

By Marion Fitzgerald

I CAN'T remember why it was first suggested that I should interview Mrs. Stephen Behan. Perhaps her son, Brendan, had been particularly in the news. Perhaps he had made some comment about her influence on him. Perhaps the Behan family, father and sons, were all coming so much into the limelight that it seemed natural to wonder about the woman behind them.

I don't remember what kind of woman I expected to meet. But I do remember coming away from the meeting completely enchanted – and sure that Mrs. Kathleen Behan must be the greatest Behan of them all. Her vitality, her obvious and bubbling zest for life, her complete lack of affectation, made her seem the kind of person you could warm your heart at – an opinion that hasn't changed over the years. That first interview was in December 1962 – when the whole family seemed to burst out in the flower of genius – and much of what we talked about then is relevant to the picture of Brendan and the way of life he was used to.

I asked her about her sons. She had seven but the last one died. 'Six grew up. I used to rejoice that I had six sons to carry my coffin to the graveyard. Now that's over. Now they bring the coffin in the hearse to the graveyard. I have one daughter. I always say that we are seven, like the poem in the book. Rory is the eldest. He's married with his own kiddies,' she said. 'Sean is next and he works in London, and he's an electrician or an electrician's helper would be more like it. Seamus is an electrician in Selfridges. They all have very nice jobs. Brian is a carpenter and he lives in Herne Hill, near Brixton. Dominic is in London.

'Carmel is married too. But they were all home for the day when the B.B.C. did "This is your life". They brought a brother of mine home from America . . . a lovely time we had.'

The recorded programme of 'This is your life' was due to go out on that day in 1962 when I first met her. She and her husband were going along to one of their favourite pubs to see it; they hadn't – and still haven't – got a television set themselves, 'because if we had it, Da would say "Kathleen can look at the television", and he'd go off. I prefer to go with him.'

Brendan was the eldest of Mrs. Behan's second family. 'I was

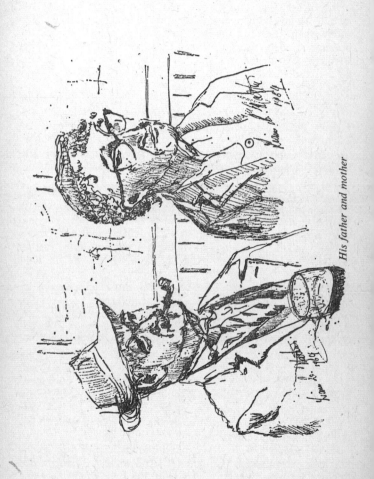

His father and mother

twice married, you know. I was left a very young widow. I was only two years married to Jack Furlong, a 1916 man. I was staying with his mother and Stephen used to visit there and that's how I met him. Rory and Sean are Furlongs.'

But of her large family, none are now at home. 'Da and I are here all alone and it's very lonely. I can't bear to go to the back room where the boys used to sleep. They come home for the holidays though – and we spent three weeks in London once. Brendan gave us the money to go. Dominic gives us whatever he can and the others give us what they can. They're all very good boys.'

She asked me if I had ever met Da – her husband? 'You'd love him if you did. He's very jolly, though he's as quiet as a lamb. I never heard a cross word from him in the forty years I'm married to him, excepting I raised it myself.'

She poured us both glasses of cider, which she produced after hunting round a cupboard for a bottle 'that should be there unless Da got at it'.

I asked her if she found it hard, rearing seven chidren? 'Yes, we had a hard enough time. Da was 15 years in a job when I married him, and then he was made a political prisoner and when he came out the job was gone. He'd get a job for a couple of days and then be knocked off for a couple of days. But he always worked when he could get it. And we gave all the boys a trade which was a hard thing to do. Da's mother owned slums in Russell Street and we didn't have much rent to pay. Da would never have moved out of there. He hates moving anywhere. We only moved out of Russell Street after it was condemned and nearly fell down on us. We're over 20 years out in Kimmage now. When all the boys left I'd have gone to a Corporation flat – but you couldn't move Da.'

While it may have been hard at times to make ends meet, Mrs. Behan didn't feel that the young Behans had been hard boys to rear. 'All boys are wild, but they were no wilder than any other boys. They always worked when they got it – they had to. The greatest trial was when they left us and went to live in England, and left us here alone.

'Sean joined the R.A.F. We didn't like the idea of him joining anything except in his own country. And when the papers used to come for him, I used to burn them. But one day he went and met the postman and wrote off and joined up. It didn't do him a bit of harm. He's a pension out of it now. The others worked on the unemployment platform here. That's how they had to leave Dublin.'

The young Behans thought up various ways of making money. 'Dominic and Sean got a brilliant idea that they'd sell turf and they managed to get £100 between them. But you'd want to be reared to that and Sean is a bit of a gentleman in his own way. The poor people were glad to get the turf and meant to pay for it, but when Dominic went back on a Saturday to collect the money they wouldn't have it. They lost all the £100 and the horse got killed. Now the people around say – when they want to take me down a peg – "I remember your sons selling turf". And I say if they got paid for it they'd be well away.

'Do you know, when Dominic was four years old he fell into the Canal near Russell Street! Only his little boots were up and a neighbour plunged in and saved him. It was a basement we had and somebody came to the railing – Carmel had only just been born – and said "Dominic is drowned". But he wasn't, though he spent a week in the Mater Hospital after it.

'Another day – Da never brought out the children, that wasn't in his line – but one day he came out with us and we were walking across the Bull Wall with the seven of them behind us. Suddenly we looked round and he said, "Where's Brendan?" There was no Brendan. You know the big holes left by the bombs? They were covered over with grass and Brendan was down one of them with grass all over him. But he didn't die that time.'

When I asked her about Brendan and Dominic's writing talent she was very quick to emphasise that *all* her children had talents and that Brendan and Dominic weren't the only ones who could write. 'Brian and Sean write a little too, but they hide it. I believe they have written a book or two only they didn't let them be seen.' Since then Brian has proved her right with his well-received book.

'Where did they get their talent from? All my children were fond of reading. And my brother, Peadar Kearney, wrote our National Anthem. I suppose it was in them. But they didn't get a lot of schooling once we came over here to Kimmage because they had to change from one school to another and it upset them terribly. They were all clever children. I never made favourites of any of them. They were all the same to me, although people think Brendan was a pet of mine, but he wasn't.

'Da's mother – Stephen's mother – petted him a terrible lot, but I didn't. Brendan is very like his father in appearance, but I'd say he takes after my brother, Peadar Kearney, but of course Da is intelligent too. He takes after both sides of the family. I never had any hopes of any of them being writers. And I have always been happy because although they write, they have their trade if anything ever happens them. They'll never be poor. It's a great thing to have a trade.'

Brendan started writing when he was still in the Infants School, Mrs. Behan said. 'Because Sister Monica – did you ever hear of Sister Monica? She was fifty years in North Williams Street. She loved boys and she loved Brendan. I remember going down to her to complain to her of Brendan being naughty, and she said, "Mrs. Behan, are you aware you are rearing a genius?" And I didn't care whether he was a genius or not if he was good. She was very sad when I cut his curls off: he had lovely brown curls. When she died, all Dublin turned out. She had reared hundreds of Dublin boys. She was a wonderful woman, and Brendan never forgot her.'

Mrs. Behan said she liked 'The Hostage' best of all Brendan had written. ' "The Quare Fellow" was a bit foreign to me, but I liked it all the same.'

During Brendan's life-time his various exploits were reported exhaustively in the newspapers. I wondered how his mother felt when he got himself into some new trouble. She put her reaction simply enough, 'I feel very unhappy,' she said after one exploit, 'all I can do is pray for him'.

She said that Brendan was very like herself. 'I have a jolly side but I have a very sad side too.' Brendan, she felt was very much like this. 'One day he'd be leaping over the moon and the next day he'd be down in his boots. But Da is always jolly. He doesn't understand moods. I never took to drink. Da likes a drink and Da's mother used to drink a lot. I like the atmosphere of the pub more than the drink, but when I do drink I like a drop of the "crature" because it doesn't make me sick. I can take one bottle of stout but not another.'

The drink she remembers most with Brendan was champagne. He loved calling for it and 'loved the pop of the cork'. He began his drinking, as far as she can remember, about the age of nine. 'His grandmother used to give him a glass along with the rest at funerals. My brother drank a lot, too. But despite all that, do you know I was ashamed of my life in London when I saw the Irish boys singing "The Rose of Tralee" outside the doors and they were stocious.'

Mrs. Behan was young when national fervour was at its height. Her first husband was, as she put it, 'a "16" man'. Her second husband, Stephen, was a political prisoner. By contrast the young people of Ireland today must naturally seem somewhat apathetic in their nationalism. Certainly, 'they are not as national as when I was young. The national feeling seems to

41

be fading away. We went to a ball the other night, and there was not one Irish song sung during the whole evening. There were no high-caul caps or sixteen hand reels or eight hand reels. They were doing the twist the whole night.

'We were cradled in the movement. I could recite every word of "Who Fears to Speak of '98" when I was seven years old every word of it. We were reared differently you see. I remember when I was a young girl I used to meet John O'Leary. He was an old, old man, and often in George's place of an evening he'd stop and tell me about the Fenians, about prison. I knew him well.

'And I knew Madame Maud Gonne MacBride. When I was a young widow I used to be receptionist for her on her "At Home" day. Madame was very kind, a lovely soul, but one day she came to me, "Kitty," she said to me, "I have some work for you to do." So I said, "Thank you, Madame." I thought it was to scrub out some offices, and I was delighted because I was a young widow with two small children.

' "Yes, Kitty," she said, "I want you to sit for an artist." I was very ignorant at the time, and I said "Me, Madame! I couldn't sit for an artist. I'm awful looking." "On the contrary, Kitty," she said, "you're quite pretty." So I sat for Sarah Purser for a couple of years. Did I like it? Well I was paid for it, and that's the main thing. No, I don't know where the pictures are. Da was often trying to find out.'

I asked her what she liked to do in her spare time – did she like reading, the theatre, television? 'Well my eyes are too bad for reading. They've been bad ever since I was a child with the measles. Da reads for me. He reads Dickens, Willie Rooney, I know all his poems, of course. And "Knockagow". We very seldom go to the theatre. We saw "Red Roses for Me" in London and I went to "The Rose Tattoo". I didn't like it. But I liked Sheelagh Delany's "A Taste of Honey". My eyesight's too bad for me to look at much television. And anyway we haven't got it. I like knitting. Do you know, I have finished a mitten while I was talking to you. I knit all the socks for Da. Brendan liked them handknitted too. The others wear nylon. You see I can knit without looking at it, so it doesn't hurt my eyes. I like cooking – beefsteak and kidney pie, apple tart. I like to roast a little chicken for Da.'

Mrs. Behan and her husband go out for a drink on Fridays, Saturdays and Sundays. 'Da and myself, we take a little drink, we meet friends, and talk and laugh.'

'So far I have danced through life,' she told me – and it was easy to believe her. She mentioned a party she had gone to once in London where 'we enjoyed ourselves so much – I wasn't drunk – that if somebody mentioned China I would sing a song about the place, and no matter what anybody mentioned I'd sing a song about it. They said they'd send over for us for the next party. Dominic was put in the shade that night', she said with a certain reminiscent satisfaction. 'Of course, Da sang too. Peadar taught me all the songs, and I taught all the songs to the boys that they are singing now.'

The money people were paid for merely 'singing songs' as she put it, clearly amazed her. 'Do you know we got £25 from the Canadian Broadcasting people,' she told me once, 'and all we did was sing a few songs around the fire in Dominic's place in London.'

Basically she is a very buoyant person. 'I must have been born happy and I must have been born singing. I'll be singing a song when I'm dying, an old "come-all-ye".'

In fact, she will sing a song at the drop of a hat. 'Last night we were in a pub down here locally, and they were all talking about cats and dogs. They only allow us to sing on Friday, Saturday and Sunday, but when they were talking about the dogs didn't I sing "My daddy wouldn't buy me a bow-wow". We had the best of laughs. It's an unheard of thing to sing on a Monday night. But I sang, though I shouldn't have been singing at all. We'd be barred, ruined, only that we were in a little room to ourselves.'

The best of laugh and the best of life is what Mrs. Kathleen Behan has obviously made for her family – and anyone else who has had the good fortune to come into contact with her.

3

THE REBEL

By Anthony Butler

THE image of Brendan Behan the Rebel was completed when they buried him. All the traditional ceremony was provided. The National Flag draped the coffin: he had a Guard of Honour of his old I.R.A. comrades and at the last poignant moment a Fianna Boy Scout in his military-style uniform sounded the Last Post and Reveille.

The pure patriot, the idealistic gun-fighter, the socialist, the enemy of cant and hypocrisy, the great-hearted drinker, the unconventional genius – it was a fine and stirring memory for those who mourned for him in Glasnevin Cemetery. And there were many to weep.

The President of Ireland was represented; members of the Government attended and the Lord Mayor of Dublin was also present. Poets and trade unionists, playwrights and priests all gathered to pay tribute. No other funeral in recent years had brought together such a representative selection of Irish life. A cynical friend of his remarked: 'There should be a leprechaun with a wreath of shamrocks'.

The oration at the graveside – the customary tribute of Irish Republicans to their dead leaders – was given by Mr. Matthew O'Neill and his sincere and moving tribute underlined once again the popular concept of the dead man.

' . . . they could still hear the echoes of the fine baritone voice singing "Wrap up my green jacket in a brown paper parcel; I won't need it anymore". Brendan Behan would want to be remembered for his secret drillings and parades, his daredevil exploits, his time in Borstal and imprisonment in England and in "homely Mountjoy", Arbour Hill and Tintown and the Curragh . . . patriotism and republicanism were the subjects on which Brendan based most of his writings.'

The obituaries and the flood of articles which followed his death re-touched the picture with stronger colours and the chorus was almost unanimous. A prominent Dublin broadcaster described him as a revolutionary and claimed that he was always opposed to the accepted rules of society. Seamus G. O'Kelly, a Republican writer asserted that Brendan was in the Fenian tradition; Flann O'Brien the author of *At Swim Two Birds* called him a fearless denouncer of humbug and pretence. In another notice he was praised for his tilts at the Establishment.

If anything would appear to have been certain in the wayward and extravagant existence of Brendan Behan, his right to be considered a Rebel would thus appear to be unquestionable. But is it a true picture of the man and should it be allowed to stand as an ultimate judgement?

There is sufficient reason to reject it. In the first instance the Image resolutely refuses to fit into the factual framework of his life. Almost immediately the concept of the Rebel is distorted by the presence of the entire Establishment at his graveside – religious, literary, political and social. True rebels seldom earn so massive a tribute.

Again and again the contradictions split the conventional picture and the two and two of reality will not add up to the five of myth. A mask seems to slip revealing evasive subtleties and shifting variables.

Some extraordinary conclusions emerge from serious analysis. Where his deepest and most felt ambitions were involved, for example, he could be – to employ his own vocabulary – an 'arse-licker', a sycophant who selected his posteriors with the assured discrimination of the artist. For he had ambitions – vast and dynamic – and a full appreciation of the genius he possessed.

In rejecting the popular idea of Brendan Behan there is no need to debunk him in any cheap and paradoxical manner. If anything is involved it is a promotion rather than a debunking. In the end, it may be claimed, the true and essential man was a damn sight superior to the coarse trigger-happy buffoon with the big heart and the open hand which the world at large accepts he was.

The repute of Brendan as the Patriot Rebel rests mainly on his youthful exploits as a member and at times a near-member of the Irish Republican Army. There is no doubt that as a boy he was devoted to the ideal and to the service of the Irish Republic. A poem of his published in 1938 expresses orthodox but passionate nationalism and it is also distinguished by a literary skill unusual in a lad of fifteen.

In those pre-war days Republicanism was a flower that blossomed widely and the arms and ammunition to nourish it were plentiful. I know of one mother who found nothing peculiar in celebrating the twenty-first birthday of her son by the presentation to him of a Colt .45 in a velvet-lined case. On another occasion visiting a friend of mine in the movement I discovered that my discomfort on his sofa was caused by a .32 automatic in the stuffing. As a gesture of contrition he offered it to me for thirty shillings.

In 1938 the I.R.A. was recovering from the divisions which weakened it after the outbreak of the Civil War in Spain. Those who seriously supported the Spanish Government were now fighting outside Madrid in the International Brigade.

A General Convention of the Army was held early in that year and a resolution was passed that the time was opportune once again to attack England, the oppressor of Irish freedom. The preparations for this assault were thorough and ingenious and the development of what was called an Expeditionary Force required a good deal of training.

With an old world courtesy, that was not fully appreciated, the I.R.A. sent an ultimatum to the British Government and warned that they must leave Ireland's northern six counties or take the consequences.

As the note stated: 'The Government of the Irish Republic believe that a period of four days is sufficient notice for your Government to signify its intention in the matter of evacuation . . .'

It will be noted that the elected Fianna Fail Government in Dublin was treated by the I.R.A. as non-existent. The British however considered the warning to be a practical joke or the work of a lunatic and ignored it.

When they showed no sign of leaving, the campaign commenced with the blowing up of Customs huts on the border between the two parts of Ireland. In January 1939 it spread to England and in January of that year transformers and other public utility equipment were the object of widespread attack and damage.

Brendan, although he was not yet sixteen, was in the I.R.A. itself and in the training programmes at Dublin's lovely suburb of Killiney he proved an expert with explosives of all kinds. One of his friends of those days told me that he was without fear in handling dangerous substances. Indeed when Brendan gave a lecture on one occasion he alarmed his 'pupils' by lighting matches and throwing them at the explosives.

Early in 1939 he was in London assisting in the manufacture of bombs and in December of that year he slipped over to Liverpool to make it a noisy Christmas along the Mersey. There is every reason to believe that this was an independent effort – a private Behan war against England. It was not to be successful.

On the day he arrived he was checking over his stock of explosives when the detectives burst into his room in a house on

Aubrey Street. At the moment they arrived he was taking acid from a bottle in his suitcase with a glass fountain pen filler. When the room was searched sixteen toy balloons were found and twenty ounces of potassium chlorate and sugar. Brendan was later to suggest that he went to Liverpool to blow up Britain's newest battleship the 'King George V'. It is doubtful if twenty ounces of potassium chlorate even when mixed with sugar would have proved sufficient for this task. Had he succeeded, however, his place in the history of naval warfare would have been assured.

The bottle probably contained sulphuric acid and I.R.A. incendiary bombs were made by injecting a small quantity into a balloon. When this had eaten through the rubber it came in contact with the potassium chlorate and sugar mixture and ignited anything in the vicinity. The simplicity of these devices enables them to be sent in envelopes through the post.

On his first brief appearance in court he stated that he had come to England to fight for the Irish Workers and Small Farmers' Republic – an assertion which must have shocked the I.R.A. staff. They had no desire to see their ideal Republic in sectional terms and certainly did not want it associated with pink politics. It was not the last time that the unorthodox Brendan was to become an embarrassment.

Early in February 1940, while the Nazis and the Allies mildly sat out the first winter of the war he was tried in Liverpool. In Ireland there was bitter excitement as on that morning two Irishmen – members of the I.R.A. – were executed in England on twin gallows. Peter Barnes and James McCormick had been charged with the murder of a girl in Coventry on August 5, 1939, when the accidental explosion of a bomb killed five people in the city.

The emotional tension in Dublin and throughout the country was heightened by the belief – and there seems little doubt that it was correct – that at least one of the men concerned had nothing to do with the incident which put him in the hands of a hangman.

Brendan was conscious of their great sacrifice and moved by it but at the same time he tells us in 'Borstal Boy' that he knew it would be looking for trouble if he made a gesture of protest. A petty Irish crook named Callan who was in jail for stealing Harry Lauder's overcoat proved less discreet and insisted on making a futile but gallant protest. Calling on Brendan to join him he shouted 'Up the Republic' and other slogans in his cell until he was battered into silence.

Whispering a very muted 'Up the Republic' in reply to Callan down a ventilation shaft Brendan slipped back to his bed before any of the warders came near him. While his sober discretion was understandable and sensible the incident does not match with the notion of a hot-blooded young rebel.

In court he is reported to have smiled when he was accused of having explosives and with a light-hearted air he informed the court that he had no interest in the proceedings. Mr. Justice Hallett who presided did not feel kindly to the cheeky prisoner and he made no secret of the fact that given the opportunity he was prepared to hand out a fourteen years sentence at the drop of a ball and chain. The uninterested Brendan shouted: 'That's a lot of damned lies' when Detective-Sergeant Earps was giving evidence and he was warned that he might be removed from court if he repeated the performance.

Reading an alleged statement by the prisoner a detective gave evidence of how Brendan informed him that the main target of his bombs was Liverpool's big stores.

'I am only sixteen,' the alleged statement went on, 'and they can't do much to me'.

Once more Brendan interrupted sharply and said that he did not make such a 'ridiculous assertion'.

Mr. Justice Hallett, reluctant to abandon a good idea without exploring all possibilities asked if there was no doubt that the prisoner was only sixteen and yearningly pointed out that fourteen years behind bars was available for adults on the charge.

When the prosecution was finally completed by Mr. Eric Errington, M.P., Brendan made a speech from the dock, a hallowed tradition of Irish nationalism – although it is usually made only by those sentenced to death or very long terms of imprisonment – and the collected addresses of patriots fill many volumes. Brendan's was a standard production with echoes of countless others but at the same time it was an excellent effort for a boy of sixteen.

'It is my proud privilege and honour to stand in an English court and to testify to the unyielding determination of the Irish people to regain every inch of their national territory, and to give expression to the noble aspirations for which so much Irish blood had been shed, and for which so many hearts have been broken and for which so many friends and comrades are languishing in English jails.'

In spite of his exasperated feelings Mr. Justice Hallett was impressed by what he considered to be the prisoner's impromptu oratory. Like so many others he was deceived by Brendan's talent for hard work when a particular effect was required. The speech had in fact been written out several times and then learned by heart. To surprise by secret and unacknowledged burning of the midnight oil was part of the Behan technique. 'Three years in Borstal', said the frustrated Mr. Justice Hallett.

To what extent we can rely on all the details in 'Borstal Boy' is doubtful but in general it seems to be a fair account which is supported in some places by independent testimony. In it Brendan makes no secret of the fact that he conformed to the rules and was a docile and obedient prisoner. The Governor of the institution has placed on record the opinion that Brendan was a very good boy who never used a single improper word in the presence of officials. He mentions how on one memorable occasion he played the organ while Brendan sang hymns. This is an early example of Brendan's intuitive rightness in selecting a method to impress a given individual.

Indeed the Governor was so impressed by the Dublin boy that he recommended his early release when only eighteen months of the original sentence had been completed. It can be stressed that no rebel would have found himself at liberty after so brief a period. He gave the authorities an assurance that he would not return to Britain on I.R.A. activities at least until the war was over and this was accepted as adequate evidence of reform. It is not a custom for Republican prisoners to compromise with their jailers and Brendan's promise was somewhat contrary to the code. It is possible to sympathise with a lad of eighteen in a situation of this kind but the contradiction in the future Image should be noted.

One incident in Borstal illustrates again his striving for effect; his awareness of what hard work can do for a writer. An essay competition was held and Brendan determined and was certain he would win. He mentions that he wrote and re-wrote, polished and amended his contribution until he was perfectly satisfied with it. No one appears to have challenged his effort to any serious degree.

He admits with amusement that his earthy and non-intellectual friends were astonished as he had not told them of his essay – he wanted to surprise them as he surprised the judge at his trial.

Not alone did he wish to do things superlatively well but he wished to give the impression that he could do them with superlative ease.

It was a harmless and beneficial vanity.

The impression he made on all of those at Borstal was summed up by the matron of the institution when she said to him:

49

'You're a very good boy, Brendan, and a real credit to us.'
But where was the Rebel?

Somehow it makes us understand and accept Dominic Behan when he describes his brother as gentle, shy and kind in those days.

When Brendan returned to Ireland in 1941 he was a marked man and his association with the I.R.A. was less formal. In the language of the organisation he 'kept in touch' and participated in several 'jobs' including one in Belfast. In spite of this some explanation is required of his violent eruption at Easter, 1942, when he shot at policemen and became the central figure in a sensational incident.

The story as told by his relations in books and articles follows a simple pattern. Brendan attends the annual march of the I.R.A. to Glasnevin Cemetery; grabs a gun from a friend and starts shooting at the police. It is a simple legend, one typical of a Rebel but in view of the facts it does not make sense to me.

In order to obtain an exact account of the incident I interviewed Mr. Andrew Nathan who was arrested with Brendan on the day in question.

The shooting did not take place at the cemetery but at De Courcy Square which is a considerable distance from the main gates. The parade had dispersed and as Andrew Nathan, Lazarian Mangan and Joseph Buckley walked along side by side they were approached by members of the Special Branch, the police section which kept an eye on the I.R.A. Detectives Martin Hanrahan and Patrick Kirwan caught Mr. Nathan by his arms and held him while Lazarian Mangan drew his gun and ran out to the centre of the road where he hesitated for a moment. Brendan Behan who had not been with any of those initially involved came up and called to Mangan: 'Use it! Use it!'

Mangan still hesitated and Brendan with a significant gesture threw off his coat and jacket and shouted: 'Give it to me and I'll shoot the bastards!' Mr. Nathan can still vividly recall the money and odds and ends rolling around the road from Brendan's discarded clothing.

Firing two shots at a range of about fourteen yards – the width of an average street – Brendan then ran further ahead before turning and firing again. He then ran away as other police closed in.

I have not relied on Mr. Nathan's account alone and a check of newspaper reports reveals that it is substantially correct. It seems to me that the throwing of the coat and the jacket on the ground by Brendan is a clear indication that he was to a large extent under the influence of drink at the time. It is the typical gesture of an intoxicated man in a condition of intense emotional excitement. In this light Brendan's intervention was hardly one for which he could be held responsible.

It is only right to record that an intimate I.R.A. friend of his doubts my theory and states that it was never suggested later that drink had anything to do with the incident. It is his belief that Brendan threw off his overcoat and jacket in case they might hamper him in running. To me it is more than doubtful that a man who is sufficiently excited to shoot at policemen would at the same time, be clear headed enough to make preparations for retreat. In any event it would have been adequate to discard the overcoat if speedy action were contemplated.

He got away for a day or two and his home on Kildare Road was visited several times by the police. They caught one glimpse of him around the centre of the city but, as they stated at the trial, it was impossible to shoot because of children. It was made known, however, to his friends and relations that he was likely to be shot on sight. Brendan gave himself up in circumstances which had all the hallmarks of a negotiated surrender, and unarmed was taken into custody.

The shooting incident occurred on Easter Sunday, April 5th, and on the 24th of that month Brendan appeared before a military court and was sentenced quickly to fourteen years on one charge and three months on another.

With characteristic good-humour he asked the presiding officer if he could take his pick as he preferred the three months sentence. Mr. Justice Hallett whose taste in fourteen year penalties had been frustrated at Liverpool had every reason to read the report of the trial with satisfied amusement. Andrew Nathan was sentenced to seven years, Lazarian Mangan to three and Joseph Buckley to eighteen months imprisonment. Brendan was not charged with being a member of an illegal organisation although the other three had to meet this charge.

Once more Brendan proved to be an accommodating and unexceptional prisoner in his attitude to discipline and the good sense which guided him well when he was free of the influence of drink kept him out of trouble.

For several reasons the I.R.A. men in Irish prisons received mild treatment and they were allowed a relative amount of freedom from retrictions if they conformed in any reasonable degree with the necessary regulations. The Irish Ministers of State had been in most cases Republicans themselves in their youth and they were stamped with the seal of the movement which remains with such men all their lives.

There is no doubt they took action against the I.R.A. with reluctance and bitter regret. They locked some of their sympathies in the cells of Mountjoy while officially they had to crush the threat to the State.

Mr. Nathan mentions that his most enduring recollection of Brendan's cell is one of books and papers scattered about it in untidy heaps. Study and writing were now the occupations of the man who was at last finding his true vocation as a writer. With the compulsive energy of a true author he covered thousands of sheets of paper with material which never saw the light of day but the practice enabled him to acquire style and force. In his mature work, under a thin filigree of obscenity, the cultured sophistication of his verbal and structural skills is obvious.

Transferred to the military prison of Arbour Hill and then to the internment camp at the Curragh, Brendan all the time improved his knowledge of Irish, extended his knowledge of world literature and employed his extraordinary memory to obtain some knowledge of French.

It would be wrong to say he was vain but he had an adequate appreciation of his own genius and talent so that long before he was released after the war his ambitions were not to be found at the bottom of a distemper bucket. With that unique skill he possessed for influencing others to help him he had already begun to inch into Dublin literary life while in the Curragh. One journalist has written how rumours came from the camp of a worker-writer – an Irish Jack London – who needed books and other tools of the trade. We can be sure that Brendan achieved this without loss of personal pride and by the most subtle and intuitive direction of attention to his needs. The secret springs of his ambition to be, not alone a writer, but a great one had begun to flow. The juvenile Rebel had almost ceased to be.

With his release he continued to keep 'in touch' but something was missing. Apart from a minor part in a rescue operation of a Republican prisoner in 1947 his I.R.A. life was over at the age of twenty-three. His abandonment of active rebellion could even be dated earlier, almost back to his release from Borstal, if my theory of his fortuitous arrest in 1942 is correct.

The reputation lingered on. It is only fair to record that his interest in the movement never flagged and all his life he continued to assist those who still pursued the Holy Grail of an ideal Ireland. He attended the funerals of all those who later died in the renewed I.R.A. campaigns of the 1950's, when spectacular raids on British army barracks in Armagh, Omagh and Arborfield showed that a new generation of Republicans had forged again a bright sword of patriotism.

In his obituary in the *United Irishman* the official Republican paper it was stated that 'he was the greatest individual subscriber to the recent resistance movement campaign and to the funds of the Republican Prisoners' Dependants' Fund. The sum he subscribed ran to four figures . . .'

In public houses Brendan would take the box from Sinn Fein collectors and after making his own large donation he would persuade with his own brand of invective the other customers to contribute generously.

When all that has been said it must also be recorded that Republicanism was, after 1945, a poor second to his literary ambitions. Anyone who thinks of Brendan as a loyal servant of the Republic should take another look at 'The Hostage'. This is one of the most derisive presentations of the I.R.A. ever to reach a stage. If it had come from the pen of any other writer it would have been denounced as viciously anti-national.

The most sympathetic character in 'The Hostage' is the young British soldier. He is an I.R.A. prisoner in a brothel and the Republican sentiments are all expressed by lunatics, whores and homosexuals. The I.R.A. itself is said to be as dead as a dodo and they are mocked for wearing the Fainne – the emblem of Irish speakers – and the Pioneer pin, a Catholic teetotaller's badge. In the final scene the I.R.A. men run away without shooting the prisoner and dress as prostitutes to escape.

Whatever justification we may offer for this play it must be made in literary terms – from the point of view of nationalism it is indefensible. It is not enough to say with Joan Littlewood that he was caught between love for and mockery of obsolete myths. There was far more mockery of the Republican movement in 'The Hostage' than love. This is not to attack Behan but to show how wrong it is to depict him as a pure rebel patriot. He was no such thing.

His work caused some confusion in the minds of his Republican friends and one or two supporters of the I.R.A. have been known in moments of private indignation to describe him as a 'chancer'. This is going too far and ignores the key fact that for Brendan everything was subordinate to the demands of his writing.

The second element in the Image with that of the Republican gunman is a picture of a horny-handed son of toil who emerges from his social level – deeply conscious of his class origin – to mock and deride the sacred cows of the Establishment. The notion of a Republican rebel has some relevance to his early history and psychological architecture but that of the social rebel is meaningless.

It is necessary to brush off the decorative pink plaster work which justifies the label of Brendan the Socialist, and it may be taken on the basis of the record that his interest in social reform was trivial. It is true he gave subscriptions to the *Daily Worker* but his generosity was always a catholic one – in the strictly non-religious sense. If asked he would probably have subscribed to the Tory party. As an economic system, capitalism suited Brendan and he boasted that he wanted to be a 'rich Red'. He had no hesitation in availing himself of its rewards and values. Alan Simpson makes the point that he was very professional in his attitude to his fees and payments. Most reasonable people will accept that he was correct in this approach but once more a contradiction shimmers beneath the Image. Certainly the system suffered no body blows from his pen and nothing he wrote could be interpreted as a contribution to the advancement of social justice. It can be stated that although true socialists may start from Anglesea Road, the upper-class Dublin suburb in which he lived they rarely end up there and remain true to their credo. His choice of residential area, in fact, is not without significance.

Perhaps the nearest expression of a social philosophy he ever attained was at the First Dublin Theatre Festival when someone mentioned to him that Siobhan O'Casey, the daughter of Sean, was a nice girl.

'Why shouldn't she be a nice girl', he replied. 'She's an effin' Communist like her father'.

He often discussed social problems in a general way with Mr. Matthew O'Neill, a friend of his who became a senior trade union official. Mr. O'Neill is, I think, most charitable when he confines himself to the statement that he was never able to pinpoint the exact attitude of Brendan to these matters.

When his brother Brian was involved in the Shell-Mex strike Brendan wandered around congratulating the pickets and abusing the scabs but again it was more in support of his relation than as a protest against injustice. But at any time he had little use for abstract reasoning and his fundamental loyalties were given to individuals and not to ideas. What his friends believed in was right and right was what his friends believed in. It is fairly certain that as a social rebel revolutionary Brendan didn't make the grade. Perhaps a partial explanation of this lies in the fact that it is scarcely correct to classify Brendan as a real worker at any period of his life.

The amount of honest toil contributed by him to the painting and decorating industry raised no peaks in the graph of production. If he gave eight years of his life – little more than the length of an apprenticeship – to the trade it was the outside limit. The truth is that he was a writer who did house-painting and not a house-painter who wrote. When this definition of profession is accepted some of the difficulties in the Behan saga are eliminated.

The evidence for this occupational orientation is to be found all through his life in prison and when he emerged. Almost immediately he began to live at two levels. On the one hand he kept in touch with all his old friends – trade and political – while taking a firm and decisive jump into what was at that time, Dublin's small Bohemian world.

This was a very wise act for a would-be writer and it was to smooth his way to acceptance and publication then and in the future. Because of the parochial nature of its intellectualism entry to the pages of Dublin's serious magazines depends much more on literary politics than elsewhere. It is useful training and the superb progress of W. B. Yeats, for instance, owed much to the school in which he learned to scramble towards success. 'Back-scratching' is often the key to progress if one may so describe it in pious charity.

It is difficult to believe that Brendan selected the ideal path to his ambitions completely by accident. To what extent 'arse-licking' may be equated with 'back-scratching' is a technical distinction for the initiated but it is safe to say that he did a little of both.

The right people were cultivated and the influential noted. His colossal sense of humour; his repertoire of songs and his fine voice; his extraordinary ability to caricature and mimic – all were employed to impress and to flatter as required. Alan Simpson notes – and his perceptive analysis of Behan has been too little appreciated – that the contacts made by Brendan at this time provided a very useful short-cut to general recognition. It was not alone an association with the doorkeepers of Irish magazines that helped but also the technical education in writing which rubbed off in many conversations with those concerned.

Soon he appeared as a writer in *Envoy* and was being recommended to other publications by names that made smooth the way. Finally, he became a columnist in the *Irish Press*, a breakthrough that gave him his first firm foothold in literature and enabled him to burn his dungarees and brushes.

The acceptance of 'The Quare Fellow' by Alan Simpson was the beginning of the real count-down to rocketing success and although the producer was too much a man of the theatre to take the play because he met Brendan in the past – once again a cultivated acquaintance proved useful to the budding author. He had looked ahead with shrewd vision.

At this time also he made a serious effort to be what he thought a playwright should be. He became conventional in dress and habits. Anyone who has seen the photographs taken during the rehearsals will note that Brendan was careful to present a shining facade for a time. There is the good suit, the neatly groomed hair and the clean shave that appears to be the result of electrolysis rather than a razor. He was on his way. He belonged.

Intensely sensitive, nervous and painfully eager to succeed the waiting period proved too much and by opening night he was a thermometer of anticipation with alcohol registering the tension level. Compared with first nights to come the Pike evening was relatively calm and he merely sang 'Red Roses for Me' in an arrangement by Arthur Guinness and Sons.

The effect on an audience, unaccustomed to drunken authors was tremendous and Brendan learned a lesson he was never to forget and which he repeated to boring tedium: 'There's no bad publicity except an obituary'.

He was on his way. He belonged. But where was the Rebel?

Soon he was to marry Beatrice Salkeld with the conventional blessing of a Nuptial Mass. We can note that although he was to state and repeat that the only people he liked were the house-painters, the taxi drivers and the bookies' runners, he took care to marry outside that social level. Neither did he choose to live in their vicinity and instead retired to the gracious suburbanity of Dublin's Ballsbridge. Some of his friends at this time noted a change in him – a desire to be 'above buttermilk' as the Irish sometimes say of a social climber.

The long hunger for recognition was over.

London beckoned and his television interview finally blasted him into the big financial orbits. Money poured in and his life was lived against an incandescent glow of newspaper reports. He became an international clown with the privilege of tapping the world with his harmless balloon – a long way from the time he filled it with sulphuric acid. For his efforts tickled; they didn't hurt.

But in spite of the drunken sensations, his arrests for minor assaults and trivial offences there was nothing of the Rebel in his conduct. It is plain that he was rigidly conformist to the needs of his public. It paid him to be drunk, singing and outrageous and obediently he served the mixture. Almost slavishly anxious to please he sacrificed his Republican ideals on the griddle of 'The Hostage' and in 'Borstal Boy' produced a great book, but one designed to flatter the British ego. He staggered through the drunken hoops held out to him and still there was no bad publicity except an obituary.

But the Image was getting out of hand as drunken bout piled on ritual sensation to create an impossible monstrosity. As Brian Behan noted he was cutting himself off from his old world. In the last four or five years of his life as he queued in the antechamber of death he began to betray anxiety that the man had eclipsed the artist. He began to stress with sad and earnest despair that he was a writer but it was almost too late.

His last books such as 'Brendan Behan's New York' are littered with a pretentious exhibitionism he would not have tolerated earlier. He drops names. 'As Arthur Miller said to me . . . Norman Mailer came up . . .' His command of French is established – an ability muted before in case it would clash with the Image and he records the manner in which he corrected a New York hostess who did not know that the nickname of the French painter Rousseau was 'Dounaire'. At the same time he contrives to draw attention to his own knowledge of art.

His growing concern with his repute as a writer was illustrated in the September 1961 issue of the *Kilkenny Magazine* in which the editor Mr. James Delahunty recorded a meeting with him.

At first there was a little jousting on tastes in food and Brendan indicates that he belongs to the 'in-group' of the gourmet as he declaims that champagne is the only drink to go with caviare or salmon. The talk shifts to writers and Mr. Delahunty notes how anxious Brendan is that his work should be accepted for its own sake and his desire to be treated seriously as an author.

It was almost too late. The Image was winning – an Image that was and is a fraud and a lie. Touch it with truth and analysis and it fades. It is a wraith made up almost completely of alcohol.

What then is the answer to the riddle of Brendan Behan?

It is probably a simple one. Its roots will be found in his ambition to be a writer; to be recognised; to be applauded. There was nothing shameful or deplorable about this although his general environment didn't lend itself to a proclamation of such an aim. It was in his case a perfectly legitimate ambition.

But when success came it had a price tag that he himself had helped to write. It seemed to demand that he should become a permanently intoxicated rowdy instead of an intermittent reveller in order to obtain and keep it. He was willing to pay the price. Perhaps his real tragedy lies in frustrated respectability for of course he was a writer and a good one.

The real Brendan – and dare it be said – the sober one was vastly different to the Image. For the moment, and possibly permanently, he is lost in the Big Lie.

There seems little doubt that he was cruelly sensitive and shy even though he was utterly gregarious. In the article from the *Kilkenny Magazine* already mentioned Mr. Delahunty records his first impression of a sober Behan and says he was a quiet, inoffensive, mild-mannered man – a little ill at ease in a crowded bar-room.

He was not alone in this experience of Brendan and it is worth quoting from a review by Brian Friel of 'Brendan Behan's Island' published in the *Irish Press*. Mr. Friel, an important Irish playwright, had never met Brendan and accepted and believed the Image. He recorded his surprise on reading the book.

'. . . we expect a swashbuckling, snook-cocking, outrageous Behan to get our goats up and wallop our sacred cows; to say all those shocking things that we think about with the reluctant half of our minds and are afraid to say in print . . . And instead we meet this mild, tame, gentle, generous-minded man who liked to lie on the rocks at Carraroe . . . or listen to stories, tell jokes or sing songs . . . All very nice and genial and ordinary . . .'

There are other sides to his life that one day a more detailed study may highlight, his poetry and his studies. Tim Pat Coogan, a Dublin journalist, said of him that: '. . . he was a good French and Irish scholar'. Joan Littlewood too spoke of him as a fine scholar and said she knew he had been translating Marlowe's poetry into Irish.

These things also deny the Image.

For all this something is owed to Brendan Behan. Reparation, justice, truth. Not alone is it due to himself but it is also the right of his young daughter who must live in the shadow of his repute as she grows up. She will be able to remember his youthful idealism and his loyal devotion to the Republic even though she may realise that his claim to be a true Rebel is a very limited one. For the rest she need feel no shame, his great kindness, his brilliant humour and his humanity. It will be enough if she can grasp the agony of the man who sacrificed so much – including probably his life – in order that he might achieve realisation as a writer. When the legends die and the stories are told she may recall him with pride, as a writer and artist. That is the way he would want it.

4

BORSTAL AND MONEY

By John Murdoch

DURING the eight to nine years that I knew Brendan Behan I had many opportunities of seeing him in action without his mask.

We all have our masks to some extent but Brendan's had a deep and sharp cleavage, almost strong enough to suggest schizophrenia. We had the drunken, rowdy, bloody, boisterous and bombastic; the Brendan Behan with the bawdy tongue. It was the side of Brendan's nature that the public everywhere knew so well, too well, in fact. For every time he was in the police court for being in a drunken fight or in a rollicking drunken scene on television, millions knew about it. To them it was the typical Brendan Behan, the wild Irishman. It was the only side of him they knew and, of course, they could hardly be blamed for that.

Only a comparative few knew the other side of Behan's character, the good Christian side for which there was no publicity. It was far removed from his rough language, the four-letter words that he used so often and his generally lamentable behaviour in public. Most of the ostensible Brendan Behan which his critics have described as his public exhibitionism has brought him discredit, but the surreptitious, unobtrusive Behan displayed his kindly, charitable nature.

For his public behaviour Brendan Behan had so many harsh, sanctimonious critics that to me it was refreshing to meet one man who probably knew him better than anyone anywhere. He was Mr. C. A. Joyce who had known Brendan for twenty-five years. For Mr. Joyce was Governor of Borstal when Brendan came under his care in 1939 at the age of 16 years. They struck up an immediate friendship which was maintained consistently from that first meeting until Brendan's death in 1964. Now in retirement at Ryde in the Isle of Wight, Mr. Joyce has spent all his working life looking after prisoners. He has studied many thousands of them and his shrewed unsentimental views on the ex-Borstal boy must carry a lot of weight in any retrospective appraisal of Brendan's character and his place in society.

It was while Brendan was in Mr. Joyce's custody 'that he gathered the material for his autobiographical 'Borstal Boy', which has been translated into a dozen languages. But 'Borstal

Boy' was banned in Ireland and there was a storm of protest in Australia when it was banned there, too.

When I went to Ryde to see Mr. Joyce a couple of weeks after Brendan's death, I expected to see a tight-lipped harsh looking individual whose life of being tough with the toughest criminals would be reflected on his face and in his general personality. But instead I was greeted at the gate of his cosy little roadside cottage by a big, handsome genial man with a kindly face. There was nothing about Mr. Joyce to suggest harshness or prison life. A becoming head of steel-grey hair; a big round face with pink baby cheeks; a ready smile; soft blue eyes and a jovial manner.

Mr. Joyce, a keen psychologist of the criminal classes, had forty years of practical study. But he did not regard Brendan Behan as a criminal. He was just a mixed-up kid.

As we sat in his study talking about Brendan Behan, Mr. Joyce's huge broad-shouldered frame filled his swivelling office-desk chair.

'Brendan Behan came to me towards the end of 1939 to serve a three year sentence,' began Mr. Joyce in slow matter-of-fact tones. 'I was impressed by him immediately. I did not, of course, treat him any differently from any other prisoner but he struck me has having a high sense of humour, an exceptional degree of honesty and quite unusual intelligence. His intelligence showed itself mainly by his approach to problems; his extraordinarily sharp and quick wit and the colourful choice of words in his ordinary speech. In ways he was so refreshing, so out of the ordinary.

'To start with the end of his sentence first. I recommended that he be released after 18 months. He was duly allowed to go free to return to Ireland or to stay in England if he wished. But I recommended that he be released only after he had given me a definite promise that he would not attack my countrymen as the I.R.A. had been doing in 1939 in England. I said to Brendan, "You know we are already fighting one enemy. Do you understand?" The humour and wit of his character came out like a flash when he said, "Sure, I promise not to do anything until we have done with this bastard Hitler and after that I can always consider it again, can't I?"

'I told him that while he loved his country, I also loved mine and I had to play my part in its protection. He understood my point of view perfectly.

'Then I was amazed to read in the newspapers that Brendan, before the war was over, was sentenced to 14 years imprisonment in a Dublin court for attempting to shoot two detectives.

I could not understand this because when he was released from Borstal I trusted him. Unexpectedly, I got a letter from him at a time when I thought he was still in prison. He wrote: "I didn't break my promise. I snatched the gun from a fellow who was going to use it on the detectives and when I was arrested it was, of course, found in my possession."

'Whether Brendan's statement to me in that letter was true or not I am not going to say, one way or the other,' added Mr. Joyce, 'and I want to make it perfectly clear that I am not suggesting that the police framed him. I am merely giving the blunt bald statement as I got it.'

Mr. Joyce saw much on the 'positive and creditable' side of the playwright's character.

'Most people will be surprised to know that Brendan Behan was an intensely religious young man. But he did not wear his religion on his cuff. It was deep down in his soul, fundamental and solid. He came to me as a member of the I.R.A. and as such, he was excommunicated. That worried him a great deal because he was not allowed to attend Mass. He came to me one day and said: "You must understand, sir, that the freedom of Ireland is to me a second religion. I was bred to believe in it and work for it." And very often he would come to me and say: "Governor, couldn't you persuade the Father to let me go to Mass for I feel all lost without its consolation." I knew that the priest was helpless in the matter. He was merely acting on the instructions of his Bishop. But to satisfy Brendan I did ask the priest and he explained. Brendan was very sad when I told him.

'Then I said to the boy: "Listen, son, I am not a Roman Catholic but I would like to go to Mass with you. We'll sit together. I can't receive it for one reason and you for another, but we will pray to the same God together, Brendan." And we did.

'Sometimes we would go into the chapel together when nobody was there. I would play the organ for him. We sang, "I'll Sing a Hymn to Mary" and "Sweet Sacrament Divine". I have no doubt at all that Brendan was a good boy at heart and he loved his religion.'

Mr. Joyce continued: 'I was not interested in whether the boy was in the I.R.A. or not. I saw there was much good in him if only he would give himself a chance. I was not interested in his past but in his future. As a Governor, I was always more interested in rogues than in roguery. I regarded Brendan as I did the other prisoners – not just a number but a man with a soul, a living human being.'

Ex-Governor Joyce said that the Dublin playwright could not

have used the bad language in Borstal that he claimed to have used, in 'Borstal Boy'.

'This claim was just an aspect of Brendan's character. It was merely a pose, all part of the mask that he wore even in Borstal. He appeared to be a loudmouth aggressive type but at heart he was a kindly soul. In his book, he described incidents retrospectively and put in the lurid language as part of the colour to make, what he thought, was good reading. We were not unreasonable in regard to bad language in Borstal in my time. If somebody said, "bloody stupid", or something like that nothing was done. But four-letter words were certainly forbidden. Brendan never used them. I remember on one occasion he apologised to me for using bad language. He said he was not aware that I was present. But I did not hear what he was supposed to have said. I always found him kindly, charitable and generous. He loved his mother and his country.'

Mr. Joyce said that Behan and he never lost touch with each other over the twenty-five year period until Behan's death. Frequently Brendan phoned him at one o'clock in the morning for a friendly chat from Dublin.

'The last time he phoned me at that hour my wife answered', said Mr. Joyce. 'She said: "Brendan dear, will you go back to bed and phone about ten in the morning." And in his rich Irish voice he replied, "shure that is drinking time in Ireland". Whenever he phoned at one in the morning he usually explained that, to use the jockey's language, he was "under pressure".'

Brendan Behan and his old Borstal boss corresponded a lot and Brendan's mother wrote a couple of letters to Mr. Joyce thanking him for the kindness shown to her son while he was in Borstal. For many years after his release, Brendan sent Mr. Joyce lovely Easter cards expressing highly religious sentiments and scribbled inside 'with fond remembers to the "Old Man" and Mrs. Joyce; see you in Church'.

At his home in Ryde, Mr. Joyce was saddened by the death of the Irish playwright. 'He was one of the most lovable characters that ever passed through Borstal,' said Mr. Joyce, 'no matter what he did you could not help liking the man.'

I played an indirect part in having 'Borstal Boy' published. Brendan had tried various people without success and he asked me to read it in typescript during Horse Show week in 1956. The uncensored version was much more hilarious and outrageously funny than the final product. For Brendan found it difficult to restrain either the written or spoken word. He never wrote to please or displease anyone and he was not interested in making an impression. It must be said that in that first typescript of 'Borstal Boy' there was a superabundance of oaths and swear words but no blasphemy. On one page I counted a certain four-letter word twenty-six times.

As a work of its kind this autobiographical novel was a masterpiece and the cleaning up process did not detract from the merit of the story. I wrote to Charles Eade, Editor of the *Sunday Dispatch* in London recommending that he should serialise 'Borstal Boy'. This was done and the series appeared in September and October 1956, bringing in a substantial weekly cheque to Brendan at a time when he was really hard-up. Fortunately for Brendan, Charles Eade did not fully appreciate the public appeal that 'Borstal Boy' would have and he published it only in his Irish edition.

About a year later it was suggested that Brendan should try selling the same story to *The People* because the London executives of that paper were not aware that it had already been serialised in the Irish editions of their rival. This idea worked and the Editor of *The People* ran the story in all editions. This not only meant a substantially bigger cheque for the author but it also attracted the attention of London publishers. So 'Borstal Boy' appeared as a book with tremendous success in 1958. As a writer, the Dublin house-painter had arrived. He painted and papered no more although he retained his trade union card right up to the time of his death.

Delivering the weekly cheque to Brendan for his 'Borstal Boy' series in the *Dispatch* gave me an opportunity to see another aspect of the author's mental make-up. The cheque was sent to me from London to be handed to Brendan because at that time he had changed his address to a basement flat in Waterloo Road. I made three such deliveries, gaining much in experience in the process but on the discredit side, suffered much from a shocking hang-over.

Beatrice, his wife, was not at home and there were empty bottles and tumblers all around the kitchen, on my first visit. Brendan had been entertaining some of his cronies and a good time appeared to have been had by all.

It was about noon on a bright sunny morning when I knocked and the response was a deep raucous voice to 'come in'. It was Brendan's voice and it sounded throaty, dry and crackling. 'Come in', he roared again when I was in the kitchen. The voice came from a small darkened room off the kitchen. There I found Brendan in bed in his shirt. The bedclothes were tossed into a heap on one side and some were on the floor. Brendan laughed and broke into 'The Bold Fenian Men' as he lay in bed. I could see that several upper teeth were missing. He was quick to explain that this was due to the ordinary process of dentistry and not through being involved in a fight.

Despite the hilarity and the good humour, Brendan was obviously suffering from an excruciating hang-over; his half-closed eyes were slightly bloodshot; his face was flushed and he gave occasional groans. But when I produced the envelope with the cheque, it had an electrifying effect on the patient. Brendan was certainly not an avaricious person, but he clutched the cheque like a hungry child grabbing a crust. With a bound he was out of bed. Within seconds he had his trousers on; stuffed his sockless feet into laceless shoes without stooping and threw on his jacket as he was leaving the kitchen. Unwashed, unshaved and with an open-neck shirt, he grabbed me in a vice-like grip by the elbow and within a couple of minutes we were in Searson's of Upper Baggot Street.

Searson's it had to be because Brendan was barred from the nearby Waterloo House and from Devine's at the corner and Mooney's opposite did not cash cheques. Resistance on my part would have been as impossible as trying to stop Niagara Falls.

Brendan breezed into the pub like a king, distributing greetings in Irish and in English to imbibers all around. He stuffed the cash for his cheque carelessly into his pocket without even counting it. Brendan called for a pint in a cheerful mood. Presumably not to waste good drinking time and to keep things moving, he called for a glass of malt while waiting for the pint to be pulled. It was a matter of slick timing. Brendan had knocked back his glass of whiskey and had broken into a bar of a rebel song when the overflowing pint glass of Guinness arrived.

He had a voracious appetite for hard-luck stories. Within fifteen minutes he was called aside by three different characters for a whisper and each time he parted with folding money. There was no haggling. When I left in response to a phone call, Brendan was entertaining a whole party. He was in an uproariously funny mood; singing songs; reciting ballads; telling amusing stories of his Borstal days, mimicking Irish and English accents – and buying drinks.

That became a regular Behan routine until an argument started and then it happened so often that fists would fly and Brendan would be unceremoniously thrown out and told not to come back. Until he became famous as a writer, he was barred from entering many pubs in Dublin. But when Brendan became internationally known many of the publicans regretted their action. Several of them tried to induce him to return for Brendan always had the money when he had established himself as a writer and his entertainment value attracted customers.

When the next 'Borstal Boy' cheque arrived, I had to consider the matter of delivery with a little more strategy. But it happened on this occasion that I had been asked to get an interview with him as well. In Searson's I was told that Brendan had been barred. He was not in Mooney's, but walking down Baggot Street I spotted him ahead of me on the far side of the street. Brendan was sober enough. As he sauntered along he was stopped by a character with another hard-luck story with the usual result.

He handed out money to ragged shoeless children. Then he stopped at a convent and knocked. He gave money to an elderly nun who opened the door. Before reaching Larry Murphy's a woman stopped Brendan and said something in a low voice. He parted with more folding money. 'Her husband is in jail for Ireland', he told me. It was all part of Brendan's other world – the part that so few knew about, even though the recipients of his charity might not always have been deserving cases.

It was on that particular visit to Larry Murphy's that he coined a dialogue to illustrate his contempt for the boastful phony. And when Brendan used his wit to poke sarcasm at an individual or an attitude of society he could be most devastating. We were listening to an elderly character boasting about his part in the 1916 Rebellion and making exaggerated claims.

Brendan's version ran like this: he overhears remarks in a snug between two voices.

Voice Number One, gruffly: 'Where were you in 1916?'

Voice Number Two, softly: 'I wasn't anywhere in 1916; I wasn't born until 1920.'

Voice Number One, sarcastically: 'Oh excuses! Always excuses!'

He used this happening frequently in his writings.

There was a similar situation in McDaid's of Harry Street where a loud-mouthed individual was addressing imbibers on his achievements as a freedom fighter. This time Brendan had a different approach.

Exasperated, Brendan Behan got up from his seat, walked over to the individual at the counter and roared at him, 'You are far too young to have died for Ireland!'

He always had a high regard for the true Republicans and the I.R.A. men and he never ceased to help them in a very practical way when possible.

Incidentally, it has been reported in various newspapers that

Brendan was pulled in for questioning by Special Branch detectives in Dublin over the sensational raid on the Phoenix Park Magazine two days before Christmas 1939. The report was that he had been released after forty-eight hours. This report was, of course, nonsense because at that time he was in Borstal in England.

As an international celebrity, Brendan Behan was the easiest in the world to interview, at least as far as I was concerned, and I am sure many others would share that view. The reason is simple: Brendan always said, 'Write what you like about me. You can quote me for anything.' And a lot of people did! He helped a lot, of course, with his own inimitable wit and original phrases. But there is probably nobody who could have taken more libel actions against newspapers and magazines than Brendan Behan. No such action ever occurred to him and he never complained. Or is it that he believed in Oscar Wilde's axiom: 'There is only one thing worse than being talked about; that is, not being talked about.'

Personally, I don't believe that the Dublin playwright was a publicity seeker or an exhibitionist. As far as I could see, most of his actions that brought him publicity happened quite naturally. They were not done through pre-arranged scheming or craftiness to attract attention. I could not imagine his getting drunk in order to secure publicity. And when he appeared drunk on B.B.C. television on one famous occasion, he had been locked up in a room with a bottle of whiskey before the show started. Brendan was such an unusual genius that no matter where he went or what he did, he always hit the head-lines. He was the type who made news for his name was news, just as much as royalty, for instance.

Often his behaviour was most ludicrous, even shocking. But he was not interested in anybody's reaction. That was just Brendan Behan.

I have in mind the day I went to interview him with a photographer at his home in Anglesea Road. It was two o'clock in the afternoon in mid-July and there was bright, warm sunshine.

Only a few seconds after I had knocked, Brendan opened the door and he was stark naked! He had been in the hall and he shouted with a cheerful toothless grin, 'Hold on just a minute 'till I get my trousers!'

5

IN PRISON

By Sean Kavanagh

THE Brendan Behan who arrived in Mountjoy Prison in April 1942 was a slim, good looking youth of 19, five feet eight and 130 pounds. He had been released from Borstal in England only a very short time before so he was in very good physical condition.

His arrival in Mountjoy was awaited with not a little interest owing to the circumstances of his arrest. He was captured in De Courcy Square near Glasnevin after a gun battle with Special Branch detectives (in which nobody was hurt) following the discharge of a volley of revolver shots by himself and a couple of other I.R.A. men at a commemoration ceremony in the cemetery. However meeting this mild mannered boy gave one a feeling of anti-climax; surely this was no desperado, no trigger happy gunman. Even the fact that a sentence of fourteen years penal servitude was imposed on him a couple of weeks later by the Special Criminal Court for attempted murder did not lessen this feeling. The better one grew to know him the more the impression grew that basically he was a very gentle person who in his senses would not hurt a fly.

During the fifteen months or so of the sentence which he spent in Mountjoy I, as Governor, got to know him very well. One could not avoid noticing his presence around the place for he was a character, a complete extrovert. Gay, witty, amusing, always in good humour, and his strong voice with its slight stammer, could often be heard above all others in the exercise yard or from one of the 'D' Wing landings.

When he began to write, which he did almost immediately, he came to see me frequently to look for extra visits or letters and for help and facilities for his writing, and, of course, I gave him all the assistance I could. His appearance on the Governor's parade was always welcome for he never failed to be refreshing and entertaining. He talked a good deal about his Borstal experiences and spoke with respect and affection of his Borstal Governor, Mr. Joyce, 'The Squire' as he was known to inmates, and his wife and told me of many kindnesses he had done him.

When he had written a few things including a play, called, I think, 'The Landlady', and some short stories and sketches, I

Mountjoy Prison

arranged that Sean O'Faolain should read them and come to Mountjoy to meet the author. I was present at Sean's first visit which took place in my office. They had a long chat during which Brendan was assured that he had undoubted talent and was strongly encouraged to persevere to continue with his writing. He continued to write incessantly while in Mountjoy and, of course, in Arbour Hill, where he and his companions were transferred in July 1943, and later at the Curragh.

When I first knew him Brendan had a good grasp of Irish from his schooldays. He must have worked hard at it in the different prisons for on his release he could write and speak it as fluently as English. Irish classes were carried on in 'D' Wing but Brendan was not one for classroom discipline and was just as likely to disturb or distract a class as to be part of it. However he improved his knowledge of it in various ways, and he must have benefited considerably from the help he got from a fellow prisoner, Sean O'Briain, a teacher and a native speaker from Ballyferriter. He had a prodigious memory and even in Mountjoy would recite long passages of poetry and prose from his favourite Irish authors.

Brendan was anything but a model of neatness and cleanliness and his cell was easily the untidiest and dirtiest in the Wing. I used to tell him that he kept the second dirtiest cell I had ever seen; the worst was that of a friend and fellow-prisoner of my own in Mountjoy in 1921 who afterwards became a T.D. and Parliamentary Secretary. He could on occasions though appear spick and span, especially at Sunday Mass – which he never missed and when going on special visits, such as Sean O'Faolain's.

He left Mountjoy, as I have said, in July 1943 and was later released in the General Amnesty of 1946. But, alas, that was not the last we saw of Brendan Behan as a prisoner. He returned in 1948 for a month for the non-political offence of assaulting a Garda. He had no kindred spirits to pass the time with now so he worked hard for the month at his old trade of painter. He was back again in 1954 when he got seven days for being drunk and disorderly. He had no longer the trim, slim figure of 1942; in the intervening years his weight had increased by five stone to 200 pounds.

In the course of his arrest his ankle was injured and he arrived with his foot encased in plaster. I gave him a blackthorn stick which I had to help him walk about and also a loan of my own copy of 'War and Peace'. He had not finished it when he had to leave; he promised to return it but somehow it never came back.

He hadn't quite forgotten about it though for a couple of years later when writing about Mountjoy for one of the English Sunday papers he remarked 'I must send the decent man back his "War and Peace". I hadn't got around to reading it myself, and now I suppose I never shall.'

Brendan's largely wasted life and cruel early death were a great disappointment to me and to many who knew him in his early days and who realised his wonderful potential as a dramatist and story-teller. He achieved fame as well as notoriety, in the ensuing years, but all that he produced was, in my view, only a small fraction in quality as well as quantity of what, in other circumstances, he was capable of.

In his prison days when he didn't need drink to inspire him he probably wrote most of his best work; he may have revised and re-written much of it later but I consider that it is to the imposed and self-imposed discipline of those four years that we owe most of what he has left us.

6

HIS WIFE

By Marion Fitzgerald

If Brendan Behan was an explosive personality, his wife, Beatrice, was his complete opposite. She is a calm, a placid person who took the somewhat hectic pace of life with Brendan in her serene stride. She is not a talkative, gregarious person.

I had met her briefly on a couple of occasions before her marriage to Brendan. She was a friend of a friend of mine. The first I heard of her marriage was the day before it, when she rang my friend and said would she like to come along to Donny-brook Church the next morning, she was getting married. And married she was, to Brendan Behan.

Beatrice is the daughter of Cecil ffrench Salkeld, the painter. And she herself had gained something of a reputation as a painter in her own right until the exigencies of life with Brendan ate into her time.

She went to school at Loreto Convent in St. Stephen's Green, and then spent about six months in the College of Art – 'because I had always been interested in painting. But I had to earn some money so I went to work as a clerk, though I continued to go to night classes in the College for about five years.'

She then got a job in the Museum of Natural History in Dublin as a botanical assistant. Botany had been one of her subjects in the Leaving Certificate, and drawing, the other qualification, she also had. She spent five years in the Museum until she married Brendan in 1955.

'I met Brendan because he was a friend of my father's and came often to the house. I met him first when he was about 24 and I was 17 and still at school. Then he was in jail and away in France for quite a while and I only saw him now and again until 1954. I met him once on the Aran Islands. We were staying on Inishmore and he was living on Inisheer. He'd been banned from Inishmore because he locked the police sergeant up in his own cell and threw away the keys – but he came over to Inish-more one night for a party.

'Afterwards I met him a couple of times at parties in Dublin. Then at the time of 'The Quare Fellow' in the autumn of 1954, I went out with him a few times. We were married in February of

'55. At seven in the morning, because Brendan wanted to avoid publicity.

'In fact we avoided publicity so much that I didn't even tell the director of the Museum why I was resigning. I just said I was going. He asked if I had got another job. So I said yes. And he said, "Do you mind me asking you does this mean a financial improvement?" I said I thought so. Actually it didn't, because Brendan wasn't earning that much at the time: He was working for the *Irish Press*. But ultimately, of course, it did mean a financial improvement.

'We had our wedding breakfast in the Morehampton Hotel, as it was then. There were very few people, mostly friends of my own. The best man was a boy-friend of my sister's who is now painting in Paris. We didn't tell Brendan's parents about it until that evening, when we went and had a few jars with them.'

After the breakfast, Brendan and Beatrice went round Dublin in a horse-drawn cab. 'We visited various pubs. I remember we went to the Poet's Pub in Lincoln Place, and there was a fiddler outside it. Brendan loved fiddlers because his father used to play. He asked this fiddler to play "The Coolin" and he sang it himself at the top of his voice and all around the windows opened and heads peered out.'

That night they went by B. and I. to England, spent a night in London and then went on by rail and sea to France. 'There was snow in Calais, and big snowdrifts. And Paris was so cold. We booked into a hotel, and then went to call on a friend of Brendan's, Desmond Ryan, who had a lovely flat in the Rue Molière. I had been in Paris before, but Brendan showed me a Paris you wouldn't normally see: he knew it so well.'

When they came back from their honeymoon they went to live first in a flat in Waterloo Road, and then moved to another in Herbert Street. During the winter of 1958 they lived in Spain. In February of 1959 they went to Berlin for the German production of 'The Quare Fellow'. In May they were in Paris for the Théâtre des Nations; Brendan was representing Great Britain with 'The Hostage'. They were to do a lot of travelling during the next few years.

That summer of 1959 they went to Sweden, 'at the invitation of Olaf Lagerlof whom we had met in Kerry in the spring. We stayed on an island about 50 miles from Stockholm for about a month. It was very pleasant though I found it difficult to get used to daylight at three in the morning.'

In September of 1960 they were invited to America for the Broadway production of 'The Hostage'. 'We spent four months

His wife

there. Yes, I liked New York itself, but I didn't like the climate. Before we left America we went to Montreal for three weeks. Brendan was supposed to be giving a lecture which didn't, in fact, materialise. We came back to New York and then went on to San Francisco where we spent three weeks. And from San Francisco we went to Mexico.

'I loved Mexico, though the comparison between the standard of living in Mexico and in the United States was tremendous. I bought a beautiful sweater there, the equivalent of an Aran sweater here, in Aztec designs and patterns – in Woolworths in Mexico, of all places.

'Do you know I had twenty-six pieces of luggage on my way home? I don't really know where all the stuff came from – though a lot of them held books Brendan had bought, and books are never very portable. I had to pay excess baggage at every railway station on the way back from Mexico. I travelled back from America by sea. I don't really like flying. I think I suffer from claustrophobia.

'We went to Canada again in February 1961. We were in London in September 1962, and then we went to France for a month because Brendan had been in hospital and he had to go somewhere to convalesce'.

What did it feel like to be always known as Brendan Behan's wife? 'Well sometimes – though not always – you felt that you should be more of an individual in your own right. And sometimes I got tired flitting about from place to place. When I was actually on the go I didn't mind so much.

'But being Brendan Behan's wife did make it difficult to go out and about like an ordinary person. And it was the same everywhere. Brendan thought it only applied in Ireland. But it applied everywhere you went. He did a lot of television shows in America. He must have been on the Jack Paar Show about six times. An enormous number of people look at that show and even when we stopped at little places, people recognised us.'

Any spare time she had, Beatrice was giving, not to painting, but to writing her autobiography – a job not yet completed. 'Writing is very hard if you're not a writer. I find routine is the only thing. I didn't get much chance when Brendan was alive and since then I've been occupied with my house and my baby.' But she still has every intention of finishing it. 'It's about life with Brendan and the people I met with Brendan.' Life with Brendan was never dull, that's for sure.

'Yes I met very interesting people – practically all the famous

74

American writers who have been very generous and entertained us. Thornton Wilder, for instance, who knows Dublin as well as any Dubliner. He's the only man I have ever met who can quote long passages from 'Finnegan's Wake' without opening the book. He's very fond of Dublin but he said he wouldn't like to live here: it would be bad for a writer because there would be too many jealous people.

'I met Thurber who was a most entertaining and wonderful person. I met Alan Ginsberg and Norman Mailer. People in America were all fascinated by Brendan with his stories and anecdotes. I suppose that a person as natural as Brendan is a kind of phenomenon.

'In Hollywood I met Groucho Marx, and he is just as funny to sit down to dinner with as he is on the screen And I met Harpo. His curls were only a wig. Underneath he had closely cropped grey hair, and his face was very serious and sad – like most clowns.

'I met Elizabeth Taylor. She is very beautiful. She and Brendan talked and talked about hospitals. She had been in the London Clinic and he had been in hospital in Canada. At the same party – in the late Ernie Kovacs' house – I met Shirley MacLaine, who is a charming girl, and Jack Lemmon.'

But basically Beatrice has always been a home girl, who likes living in Ireland, likes being in her own house. 'Most of Brendan's work was done in Ireland. And on an ordinary day at home with Brendan I did the usual round, the shopping, the cooking, the housework. Brendan, if he was working, worked early in the morning from 7.30 to 12. Then he might go out for a walk. After lunch he went out to meet his pals and have a few drinks.'

At home Beatrice gardened, a favourite pastime, though she used to say rather ruefully that, 'just when I have the garden straightened out we go off somewhere and when I come back it's worse than ever.'

In November 1963 the Behans' first child, a daughter, was born. She was called Blanaid, after her great-grandmother on her mother's side. And she was christened, curiously enough, in the church at Westland Row where both her father and mother had also been christened. 'Brendan was born in Holles Street, though he never said much about this because he always talked of himself as a Northsider. But I used to give him a terrible jeering about it.'

The following March, when Blanaid was just a few months old, Brendan died. 'The last time I was with him, before he went into a coma, he was asking about her. When was I going to bring her in to see him? But she had a cold and I told him I would bring her when the cold was better. He had been very excited about her coming, he loved her when she came. He used to sing her Irish songs. He wanted to take her out on trips up the mountains to the local hostelries – even though she was only a few months old.'

'Blanaid', says Beatrice, 'is like my mother in looks. She has fair hair and blue eyes. She's a very good-humoured child, very placid. She can have a temper at times but it's controllable. Brendan had a bad temper when he lost it, but he didn't lose it very much either. Blanaid is reasonable. If you explain things to her, why she mustn't do something, she listens. I think children understand a lot more than people give them credit for.

'She likes paintings, bright pictures. She likes books. She can't read yet, of course, but she likes to pick out her favourite pictures in a book. I have an old painting I did once of a cat we used to have in Waterloo Road. The cat now lives with my mother, but when Blanaid saw the painting, she recognised the cat immediately.

'She is very fond of music. She dances a lot to music when she hears it, which is strange because I haven't a note. Though Brendan was musical, of course. She keeps very good time, too. I wouldn't know, but my sister Celia tells me she does.'

I asked Beatrice what of Brendan's work she liked best herself? 'Well I know his own favourite was "Borstal Boy". He was very fond of that. I liked both "The Quare Fellow" and "The Hostage" – I find it hard to say which one I like best. They are both completely different.

' "The Hostage" made a much greater impression on the world than "The Quare Fellow" because it was more universally performed. You know I heard a schools programme by accident once when I was in England. They picked out one of Brendan's plays and said it didn't matter what costumes the cast wore, any would suit it, the play itself was so universal. The I.R.A., for instance, could be the Algerian rebels in France, in Israel the Haganah, perhaps.'

'When Brendan was writing, he worked every day. When he was writing "The Hostage" he did anyway. That took him about a month to write in Irish; it had been commissioned by Gael Linn.'

What was the most exasperating part of living with Brendan? 'I think the fact that you could never be sure he'd turn up for a meal. He'd say he'd be in at such-and-such a time and he wouldn't turn up. Or he'd ring up and say he'd be late – and it would be much later. But I got cute about that. I had my own meal and left his. Or I didn't cook his 'till he came in. Otherwise I'd have had a lot of wasted food.'

She wouldn't agree that any of Brendan's success depended on his public personality. 'His escapades didn't have anything to do with his work. At least none of them were deliberate – though he was accused of doing mad things deliberately to get publicity. Brendan never did anything deliberately. Things just happened to him. And the publicity upset him more often than not.

'I suppose he acted the stage-Irishman a bit in America, but they expected it. And they encouraged it. New York was one of his favourite places. He'd have liked to live there. I think it's a wonderful city, hectic, spectacular to look at, marvellous to visit – but I wouldn't like to live there.'

Beatrice still reads Brendan's work. 'But then I know a lot of it almost by heart. I've seen the plays so often, everywhere. No, I haven't got any original manuscripts. He never kept them. He burnt them because he said he wouldn't leave anything after him. They were all typed anyway. He never wrote by long-hand.'

Since Brendan's death Beatrice has been living quietly in her house in Anglesea Road. The top part of it she has had converted into a flat because she needs the money.

'People seem to think I'm "loaded" as they say. I'm not. Not likely to be. Brendan's estate isn't wound up yet, and it doesn't look like being for years. And even when it is, I'll probably be looking for money to pay the duty, rather than getting any money out of it.

'I had to borrow money to convert the house. A writer's estate isn't like an ordinary person's. With an ordinary person you realise the assets, collect the bills, deduct one from the other and that's that.

'Brendan's case is more complicated. The *possible* royalties for the next twenty-five years have to be reckoned. This is what the Estate Office says. So that any publisher who has published Brendan's work has to give an estimate on what he thinks the royalties will be on Brendan's work for the next twenty-five years. And then duty must be paid on this estimated figure – despite the fact that it's obviously impossible for anyone to estimate accurately what way an author's work will go, whether it will go up or down. And the longer it takes to do this, the more interest will have to be paid on the estate duty. I've been told that it will be fifteen years before Bernard Shaw's estate is wound up, because of the success of "My Fair Lady".

'Candidly, I don't think there will be anything from Brendan's estate – as I said I think I will be looking for money to pay the duty. Any royalties that come in now have to be saved up to pay it. I get nothing. That's the law for authors. If Brendan had made himself into a limited company, things would have been different. This is what I suspect O'Casey did.'

There is no rancour in Beatrice's account of her money problems. But she says frankly that the house is all she has – because Brendan made it over to her as a gift. And that as well as letting the top part of it, she will probably have to take a job. 'Though, there again, I'm up against a difficulty: who looks after Blanaid while I work? She'd be too much of a handful for my mother to have all day and every day – though she loves having her.'

I asked her if she was doing any more painting, but she said between house decorating and Blanaid she hadn't had much time. She hopes to do some in the near future. She was offered a show in New York, but felt she hadn't enough work ready. In Ireland she has exhibited in the Living Art, the Oireachtas, and the Royal Hibernian Academy exhibitions. Would she think of doing some form of commercial art? 'Well, the only thing I am particularly good at in that field is botanical drawings and I think the market for them is probably limited.

'The last work of that kind I did were the illustrations for Brendan's book "Hold Your Hour and Have Another", a collection of his *Irish Press* writings. Yes, of course I would like to do more book illustrating. It's the kind of work I could do at home, and still look after Blanaid.'

When she has time, she likes swimming, reading, and cooking – as well as gardening. 'Cooking I'm particularly interested in, but it's not much fun cooking for yourself. I like cooking for other people and entertaining.'

'I'm fairly interested in clothes. Usually at home I wear slacks and a shirt or sweater. It's more economical than wearing a dress every day, unless you are going somewhere particular.' She likes wearing tweeds, has bought some clothes abroad but not a great deal. 'In America, for instance, the quality is not the same as in Ireland. In fact their whole attitude towards clothes is different. They seem to buy a dress for twenty or thirty dollars, and expect it to last only a few months and then they discard it. If I buy a dress I like I grow fond of it, and wear it more and more. In Paris, the clothes are exotic but so expensive. London is the best shopping centre as far as I am concerned.'

The last time I saw Beatrice, I asked her, with some diffidence, one last question as I was leaving. Would she think of marrying again? She said, 'Brendan always said I should. But I don't know. Brendan was the most entertaining person I ever met, and as a friend said to me, "you'd be bored stiff with anyone else".'

THE FIRST PLAY

By Mary Lodge

THE National Dailies and Evenings had been carrying references 'A play,' they said, 'by Brendan Behan, . . . "The Quare Fellow" at the Pike Theatre, for a limited run . . .'

There was some elaboration. The *Evening Press* suggested tentatively that readers of Brendan's weekly column in its sister paper, the *Irish Press*, would have little doubt as to his potentiality as a dramatist. He could, was the view, well afford to begin where Sean O'Casey had left off. All he needed was theatre workshop experience.

The *Irish Times* reminded its public that Brendan had already appeared before them as a journalist, a novelist, a poet, and in two languages, Irish and English. Now he had chosen yet another genre – drama.

His stage was to be minute, 12 ft. x 12 ft. Its setting was a converted Georgian coach house, known as the Pike Theatre, in Herbert Lane. The site was remote enough to draw the waggish comment, 'Be sure to get specific street directions, or you'll lose yourself somewhere along the River Dodder!'

But the small unpretentious theatre, brainchild of producer Alan Simpson, and his wife, Carolyn Swift, had in a mere year of existence won a reputation for discerning selectivity. Simpson Productions had achieved a certain cachet. They were exciting, stimulating, that bit different.

Explained Miss Swift, 'we saw ourselves as a revolutionary force stirring up the theatrical lethargy of post-war Ireland. The name was picked for two reasons, one as practical as the other is symbolic.' The pike, a long spiked pole used in the anti-British rising of 1798, stands for resurgence, and the terseness of the word made it perfect for advertising.

Carolyn Swift, the Pike Theatre, Brendan Behan, dramatist, they are inextricably joined. It makes no difference that he is dead and Herbert Lane quiet of an evening. A short distance away, in a simple austere office, a dynamic, versatile, English-Irishwoman, leafs through a much thumbed scrapbook and remembers . . .

How did the Pike come to having the staging of 'The Quare

Fellow?' It had been submitted to the Abbey, who rejected it, and to the Edwards-MacLiammoir Company, who weren't interested. On its rounds, however, I learnt from Miss Swift, it had been read by MacLiammoir's niece, Sally Travers, who thought there might be something in it for Alan Simpson.

The Simpsons got a copy of the manuscript eventually, and an unprofessional bit of work it was too. 'It had,' chuckled Carolyn Swift, to whom was to fall the task of editing, 'obviously been typed by several different typewriters, in varying stages of decay, on paper of dubious origin and catholic size! The construction was loose and rambling. In Brendan's mind one good gag led to another. But dialogue, and humour of that quality could not fail to hold an audience.'

Acceptance by the Pike may have been Brendan Behan's big break, but the Pike, in the person of Carolyn Swift, remembers him as its most tractable author ever. He impressed with his humble attitude to suggestion. He agreed immediately to change from one act to three, and that 'the quare fellow', Dublinese for a condemned man, and recurring frequently in the text, would not only make a more arresting title, but cost less in printing.

Prospective improvements were drafted and passed on. In a matter of moments there would be a couple of lines of brilliant dialogue, an apposite gag in each. 'And what is more,' she added with a proud affection, 'any of my phrases good enough he let stand'.

She loved him for his obvious thrill at seeing his play taking shape on a professional stage. 'He used to nudge the person sitting next to him and say, "I wrote that". While he liked to hear a full house laughing at his jokes, he wasn't interested in impressing the conventional first nighter. He wrote for the worker out on the town for an evening'. His pride, in fact, was not in the play itself, but in what it could do for people.

Other Pike dramatists with a first play on the boards considered it declassé to show any emotion. They must appear blasé, as if this was an everyday occurrence in their lives. 'And it goes without saying', commented Miss Swift, with a touch of acerbity, 'that every word is pure gold and mustn't be touched'. But Brendan Behan retained to the end his spontaneous naiveté.

Rehearsals got under way, and the Pike management set itself the task of gathering together an all-male cast of twenty-nine, reduced by doubling to twenty-one. The actors were a glorious hotchpotch of the professional, the amateur, the student. A further worry was the danger of libel. Brendan's gift for vivid reportage gave a dangerous verisimilitude to his pen portraits of the prison staff and inmates.

Indeed at the end of the run one Dublin management was to refuse the play on that ground alone, and Carolyn Swift tells an enlightening anecdote of another. 'Oh, no, they couldn't possibly consider such a play. The author's brother had worked for them as a gallery spot operator, and had been fired for selling the *Daily Worker* to the patrons in duty hours.'

Brendan enjoyed rehearsals and was a frequent attender, adored by the cast. He posed, however, according to Miss Swift, a problem in proportions, being so large and the Pike so small. Then he was given to loud roars of encouragement, 'good man yerself', to individual actors. A by-product of the lack of space in the Pike too, incidentally, was that any old 'lag' friends of Brendan's in the auditorium were overcome by the illusion of being back inside!

As the opening night drew near, the author's excitement mounted. It was all too much for him, and the remedy was obvious and there, literally, for the taking. He went on the bottle, and appeared in the theatre at intervals, as often as not accompanied by a bemused, amiable, and utterly uncomprehending boozing partner.

'And at the dress rehearsal', went on the assistant producer with a laugh, 'he had no sooner arrived than he fell asleep. I had to detail someone to sit beside him and kick him awake every now and again. He was snoring so loud that the players couldn't hear their lines.'

But it is an ill wind, and the point was well taken. On the big night, it was the task of Manager, Tom Willoughby, in between sporadic appearances as the prison Governor, and his wife Rosamund Stevens, the theatre's Public Relations Officer, to keep the neophyte dramatist in a delicately balanced state of inebriation. As Miss Swift explained, 'we had no licence in the Pike, and if Brendan got too dry, and set out to rectify it, heaven only knew how he'd come back, if at all! So the Willoughby's had a bottle in the box office and instructions to keep him happy, but upright.'

As a result, it was a docile, almost shy, Brendan who came on stage at the final curtain in response to cries of 'Author', 'Author', and hitching up his trousers, captivated everyone with a spirited rendering of Sean O'Casey's 'Red Roses for Me'. Later he was to appreciate that it didn't do his audience any harm to feel he might make an appearance. But Miss Swift considers him incapable of the deliberate publicity stunt.

Some of her first night memories may be that bit hazy. 'I don't remember too much about it', she confesses with a disarming twinkle, 'I was out in the front of the house prompting. In fact, I was hanging over the fly rail. One of the cast, it would be kinder not to mention his name, was a bit deaf and he was only happy if he could see me mouthing the words.'

But there is nothing hazy about her memories of Brendan Behan, man and playwright. The two first met in 1947 at an informal gathering in sculptor Desmond MacNamara's studio. The 'literary lion', not long out of jail, was writing short stories for *Envoy*, and the odd poem in Irish. She was a little apprehensive, 'not of Brendan himself, but that he would sneer at my middle class background, and English voice. I needn't have worried. If people were genuine, he didn't give a damn what else they were.'

The shy quickly became his friends. He went out of his way to meet them half way and make them feel at home. On the other hand, those who tried to patronise him made a big mistake. He had a fantastic facility for making them appear cheap and shoddy.

Carolyn Swift speaks of him as straightforward and sincere. She ranks his character high as a factor in the international repute of his writings. Where Dublin gags and allusions lost in translation, character delineation did not. 'He depicted in the round', she pointed out, 'no one is ever all black or all white. Personal bias wasn't allowed to interfere with objectivity. He wrote composite portraits of the people he knew, in a witty unprejudiced manner.'

She has no recollection of hearing him refer to his writing in the abstract. He wasn't one of those 'what am I trying to do' types. The form was more 'wasn't that a great success!'

Talk about Brendan Behan and sooner or later it has to come up, his exhibitionism, his drinking, and that seeming 'skulduggery' where legal contracts were concerned.

Exhibitionism and a certain histrionic quality were a part of his make-up. Miss Swift accepts this, and more important, understands it. 'He was a born actor and raconteur. He was only exhibitionist in a particular way. I have seen him for instance, when he thought no one was looking, cross the street to give a half-a-crown to a kid. He had a quality of childish innocence that drew the young to him. They felt he was a person they could play with. My own daughter, Maureen, was on a school outing when she heard of his death, and she cried all day in the bus.'

The complacent, the self-satisfied though, were there for the shaking. 'There was nothing he enjoyed more than to amble into the lounge of the Shelbourne Hotel, on a Sunday afternoon, when Dublin's prim ladies were decorously sipping tea, and say something outrageous, just to see the effect!'

Much of his drinking was for conviviality. He met his friends in the pubs and that was the social life he liked. He drank too for 'Dutch courage' before a T.V. appearance.

'Take a look at his family background', insisted Miss Swift, emphatically. 'As I see it the sole difference between Stephen Behan, father, and Brendan, son, is that, in the case of the elder, drinking capacity was limited by a weekly wage packet of about £15 and the obligation to be on the top of a ladder, painting, the next morning, while in Brendan's case, an advance payment of £200 was not unusual, and there might be no commitments for four or five days.'

Circumstances had changed, and he had failed in the adjustment. This applied as well where contracts and fees were concerned. Where, in Carolyn Swift's opinion, he might have been a perfectly competent and business-like house painter, the mechanics of big time publishing mesmerised him. Ten pounds in the hand meant far more than the promise of a stout cheque. 'Pay him in cash', she concluded humorously, 'and he would fall in with any suggestion'.

Brendan Behan, drunken, rumbustious, Dublin house painter, had his following, and the theatre was full that Friday evening in November of 1954. Amongst the audience was a nineteen year old Dubliner, born and reared. He remembers it vividly. 'I went along to that back street garage of a theatre. It was a tatty place, with coffee at the intervals, and served by those inevitable stage-struck pretty girls.

'We all knew Brendan slightly, and had some idea of his background. He was the sort of fellow, who, if he announced he was coming to your house you got a bit nervous. Later you asked Lord and Lady this to meet him!'

The Dublin of that first night he would have a Dublin of compromise. 'Today', he suggests, 'we are, or like to think we are, more cosmopolitan. At any rate opinion is not a thing to be frightened of'. He is convinced that nobody in the Pike that evening had any idea that they were in at the birth of a great play. 'They didn't know how to take it.' He said firmly, 'you felt they were just waiting for the final curtain to rush after a knowledgeable body and ask how to react!'

His theatre-goer of a decade ago was the man with a steady job. How could such a person ever hope to understand Brendan

Behan, wildly talented, but given to behaving in a crazy way, drinking, and using four letter words.

He describes the curtain coming down to shouts of 'Author', 'Author', in refined tones. 'It was that sort of audience. Simpson had a Protestant middle-class heritage. The Behan family, and the Behan pals were there, of course, but much more in evidence was the young man about town out for a lark. I saw some discerning people, and the odd literary figure or two.'

Provocative incidents I gathered were at a premium. All he could report was the effort of a fellow member of the Sandycove Swimming Club to oust him from his place after the interval, 'on the grounds that if he had to stand any longer, he certainly wasn't waiting for the end!'

And what did an impressionable young man think of that strange play? 'I was lifted out of my seat by the implacable inevitability of the death sentence. I wasn't expert enough to see the objections to the dramatic format. Structurally it was on the lines of a joke book.'

The controversial author he thought of as a kindly enough man when sober, but with a streak of viciousness that came out when he was drunk.

The professional critics were not exactly of one mind either. Gabriel Fallon of the *Evening Press* tells an entertaining behind-the-scenes tale. It appears that the *Irish Press* Editor, anxious to do his columnist proud, asked the late Dr. Lennox Robinson, Director of the Abbey, and a member of the board responsible for the selection of its plays to do the review.

Came the interval, and what more natural than for Mr. Fallon to turn to his companion with the query, 'Well, Lennox, how are you liking it?'

'My dear fellow', was the laconic reply, 'how can you possibly expect me to enjoy a play I turned down?'

And Lennox Robinson was consistent. The following morning's *Irish Press* read: 'Walter Pater has said very truly that we are all condemned to death but with an untimed reprieve.

'Again and again in poem and play and in short story, the subject of the man condemned to death and the subject of the hangman and the subject of the victim have been treated.

'Oscar Wilde treated the subject poignantly in his "Ballad of Reading Gaol"; Thomas Hardy treated the subject from the angle of the hangman in a short story, and the hangman's point of view has been simply explained in a one act play.

'In "The Quare Fellow" which had its first production in the Pike Theatre last night, Brendan Behan has taken as his theme this macabre subject – for it is macabre.

'But he treats it flippantly. Behind all his excellent vivid back-chat we should feel a shudder, a black cap, quicklime, but he never makes us tremble. A canary is going to expire from lack of water. We feel nothing more poignant . . .'

In complete contrast came Gabriel Fallon's effusion. 'An Aristotle searching Dublin for pity and terror would have found them in good measure, primed down and running over at the Pike theatre last night where Brendan Behan's first essay in drama was presented under the title "The Quare Fellow".

'Prisoner E777 may not have worn a cricket cap nor stepped out light and gay but his departure from life at a rope's end powerfully inspired Mr. Behan to write a documentary of prison life in many respects more profoundly moving and more deeply religious than Wilde's "Ballad of Reading Gaol".

'For even more than poor Wilde, Brendan Behan has a feeling for a permanence above the permanence of one human existence, and sees man's life wholly against the background of eternity. Our academicians of drama may dismiss Mr. Behan's work on the grounds of technical immaturity, may suggest cutting this and touching up that but Mr. Behan has what most of our academicians lack, an abundance of felt life, and when he finds himself technically, the Irish theatre will have found another, and I think a greater, O'Casey.

'Even when he writes didactically – and his play in essence is a plea for the abolition of capital punishment – all the qualities that go to make a great playwright keep breaking in.

'Although the pity and terror of "The Quare Fellow" are blended with a rich full-flavoured humour which at times pro-vokes riotous laughter, the moral content of the work has the power to compel immediate stillness and bend our attention toward things we give little care to in the lives of our less fortunate brethren.'

The *Irish Times* was careful. 'One of the positive qualities – and there are many – of Mr. Behan's play, is its power of provok-ing thought. Like a modern novel, it rounds off neither character nor situation, but "passes the buck" to the customer.

'The vivid sharpness of the dialogue commands attention and makes one forget, for the moment, the blurred edges of charac-terisation and motivation; it produces in retrospect something horribly true to life in its apparent pointlessness.

'There is no progression nor development of any of the charac-ters, but that is presumably intentional and they are all at least memorable.'

And the *Irish Independent* left no doubt that while the play was the finest by a new dramatist seen in Dublin for some years, it was not a masterpiece. 'It could well be', went on the criticism, 'the first essay of a great playwright still fumbling with the mechanics of his craft.

'Mr. Behan draws characters with insight and sensitivity and his dialogue – rich racy and humorous – is as authentically Dublinesque and as forceful as O'Casey at his best, and his work gives an almost Chekovian sense of continuance. His construction is weak however, and the very exuberance of his flair for dialogue and character lead him to being too diverse . . .

'When', concludes the reviewer, 'Mr. Behan develops something more of a plot than in his present work which moves simply to the death of the "Quare Fellow" and the throwing of his last letters into his grave, we may well look to him for a truly great play.'

A section of the scrapbook closes. In the words of friend, producer, editor, Carolyn Swift, 'it was the end of an era . . .' She pauses a moment before asking softly, 'Did you know, I sold the Pike the day Brendan died?'

PART TWO

Words and the Man

Brendan Behan was a huge rolling barrel of words . . . a thesaurus with a Rabelaisian flavour. In this section three writers look at his work in different ways and with different canons . . . they look at the same book and the same characters. The different lenses of their minds magnify or diminish the different aspects of the books and the plays adding up with some verbal magic to a critical appraisal that is complete and illuminating. But the written word is not all. The Behan of broadcasting and film fame is analysed too.

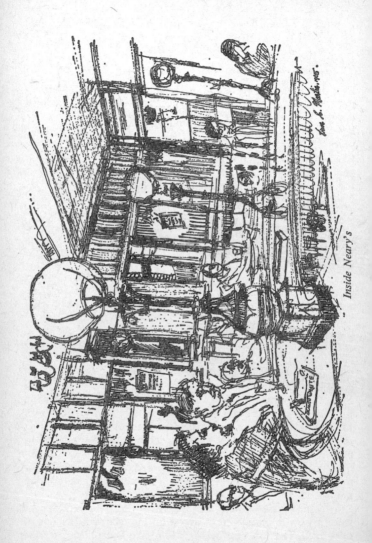

"Inside Neary's"

1

LAST PLAYBOY OF THE WESTERN WORLD

By Kevin Sullivan

BRENDAN BEHAN in his last appearance at Glasnevin Cemetery –
that was in March 1964 – drew bigger crowds than he had ever
drawn in London, Paris, Toronto or New York. 'One of the
largest crowds,' the press reported, 'seen in Dublin for many
years'. The report was heartening for Dublin has not always
treated its writers, alive or dead, with much regard – much less
with affection. There are, however, encouraging signs that
Irish attitudes are changing: the Martello Tower is now a Joyce
Museum, the Irish Tourist Board is tidying up the ruins of
Thor Ballylee for a Yeats Memorial, and there has even been talk
of a plaque for George Moore's old home in Ely Place. If the
change holds, one may yet see a public house along the quays or a
suite of cells in Mountjoy Prison dedicated to the boisterous
talents of Brendan Behan.

More than likely the change will hold, for the Irish, now that
prosperity has raised up among them a calculable middle class,
at last seem to have realised – the ad man is ubiquitous – that
their writers are as valuable an export as were, once upon a time,
their cattle or their clergymen.

This is not to say that the Dubliners who followed Behan to
Glasnevin that late March morning were in this or many other
ways deceived about the man they were burying. He was a loved
character who had been as familiar to them as the O'Connell
Bridge or Guinness' Brewery. For years he had been there among
them like a one-man slum, ramshackle and a bit rambunctious,
large of heart and loose of tongue, as direct as a fist in the face,
gentle as a decent word, without inhibitions or pretence or
perversity (barring the drink), and behind the casual no-account
obscenities of North Dublin there glowed, as Frank O'Connor
saw, the innocence of an' acolyte. This was the man Dublin
mourned for.

Of course there was a legend or myth or image or whatever the
word is now in middle-brow jargon for the factitious persona of
celebrities. That was inevitable. Behan, like Dylan Thomas, had
all the trappings that go into the making of a 'picturesque
literary figure' – a phrase that would have curdled the malt in

Behan's bowels. (I was present once when, more in sorrow than in anguish, he took the skin off the wife of a famous American writer who, with no awareness at all that she was being patronising and silly, kept insisting that he was 'the quaintest little Irishman' she had ever met.)

Soon after his first success – 'The Quare Fellow' in 1956 – he was taken up by the columnists and thoroughly lionized: here was an authentic Irish rebel ('the brave brainless boys of the I.R.A.,' Sean O'Faolain called them) who had done time in English and Irish jails for his perverse belief in the efficacy of political violence, who was a great drinker and a great talker (more monologuist than raconteur), and who was in addition the most gifted, certainly one of the most popular, playwrights to come out of Ireland since O'Casey had given the back of his hand to the Abbey Theatre. This kind of thing made good copy and Behan the journeyman journalist knew it. But more about that in a moment.

Unlike Dylan Thomas, whose public career was as brief and flamboyant as his own, Behan was until well on in life intransigently political. 'Opinions', Thomas once remarked, 'are bloody awful,' echoing in this Yeats' grim belief that 'opinions are accursed' – a sentiment surely congenial to the temperament of a poet. But Behan, though as a young man he had written a few poems in Irish – *Buiochas do James Joyce* got talked about in Dublin – was, like O'Casey, never more than a poet *manqué*. He grew up on opinions, the tough political opinions of the ferociously Republican family into which he was born at a time when his countrymen, having got rid of the English at last, were celebrating their new freedom by conscientiously murdering one another.

This insanity – a civil war delicately referred to by the Irish themselves as 'The Troubles' and by Joyce the punster as 'Devil's Era' – saw the Behans resolutely on the side of De Valera's die-hards who repudiated the treaty which made Ireland a Free State because, included in that treaty, was an oath of allegiance to the British crown. The political prejudices of Brendan Behan came into the man with his mother's milk.

He was educated, so to speak, by the Christian Brothers, a body of men more renowned for their discipline than their erudition, which would anyhow have been a commodity not in great demand in the streets of North Dublin. As a young one, Brendan and his chums (they would have been Sean O'Casey's 'chiselers' forty years earlier) would hang about after school on the corner of Great Denmark and North Great George's Street to taunt the toffs from Joyce's old school, Belvedere College, across the way.

There was nothing narrowly national about the boy's prejudices or the man's politics; his class consciousness crossed territorial boundaries, and the bricks he tossed at the tidy Belvedereans trooping out of their Jesuit school became in the days of his literacy, brickbats tossed with cuter aim at his bourgeois audiences thirty years later. For throughout his life Behan actually believed in the bourgeoisie as bogy man (his brother, Brian, joined the Communist Party – after, of course, emigrating to England – and later, when the name was famous, serialised his recantation in the *Sunday Press*), but this was like O'Casey's belief to the end of *his* life in what he thought was communism. The Irish have produced great saints and impressive sinners, but as ideologues they are, thank God, ludicrous.

Certainly there was something ludicrous about the 16-year-old boy who in the autumn of 1939 arrived in Liverpool with a Sinn Fein conjurer's kit 'containing Pot Chlor, Sulph Ac, gelignite, detonators, electrical and ignition' to bring an Irish war to England's doorstep. The British, who at the time had another kind of war to face – not at all funny – picked the lad up in a day or two and, after an awkward interval of knocking him about among more hardened criminals, packed him off to Borstal, a correctional institution for the young, and as yet unpractised, criminal.

Thus began Brendan Behan's higher education. He was to make the most of it, as his later work showed, and in this he had the help of his fellow countrymen, for no sooner had the English deported him in 1942 than the Irish slapped him back into a jail of their own until the general political amnesty of 1946.

He varied and rounded out his education during the late 1940's in Paris (study abroad appealed to him) where he acquired considerable fluency in French and began contributing articles ('pieces of pornography,' he later called them) to the Left Bank reviews, *Points* and *Merlin*, and more chastely to an Irish daily back home.

The writer in Behan was continually in danger of being shouted down by the talker, the playwright upstaged by the vaudevillian, the artist elbowed aside by the anecdotist. But at his best – in 'Borstal Boy', 'The Quare Fellow' and 'The Hostage' – he had his clowns and leprechauns, imps and improvisations, so under control that when they did appear, as they constantly threatened to do, it was at a writer's command. The trick, as Behan said, was that of the music hall where, if things got dull, you livened them up with a song and a dance 'and while the audience were laughing their heads off you could be up to any bloody thing behind their backs.'

It was, he said, what you were up to then that made your stuff great. Behan was up to a number of things.

Not surprisingly, the best things he did are all three concerned in one way or another with men in prison. Or, put more portentously, man the criminal. 'The Quare Fellow' is a savagely hilarious commentary on the idiocy, the moral hypocrisy of capital punishment in a society which prides itself, as in Ireland and elsewhere, on its moral refinement. But the tone of this commentary never betrays the underlying seriousness.

This is through a play which, though it has no discernible plot, creates a suspense, at once relentless and uproarious, from the emotional interplay – jocular, obscene, derisive or sardonic – among prisoners and their wardens, who it is clear, are no less prisoners than the men they keep watch over.

At the very end of the play, Behan for all his cleverness at concealment almost gives the game away. 'The Quare Fellow' (who never appears on stage) has been hanged, his grave dug, and the prisoners who dug it are set to quarrel over the last mortal possessions of the dead man – final letters to his family 'worth money to the Sunday papers' – which are supposed to be flung into the grave after him. Instead, they divided the spoils among themselves, tossing the last letter up in a play of chance. The identity of the Quare Fellow – and his relation to prisoners, wardens and audience – is intimated, but no more insistently than this.

And so the game is not quite given away, the tragic mask is not displayed, and the dramatic surfaces of the play are preserved intact and unspoiled. The tragedy remains as invisible as the Quare Fellow himself, in an almost pure state, so to speak, so perfectly is it encapsulated in the coarse rinds of comedy.

'The Hostage' is also set in a prison of sorts – this time improvised from a disreputable Dublin lodging house where a young cockney soldier is held captive in reprisal against the hanging of an I.R.A. man the following morning. In one sense the play can be taken as Ireland's rowdiest contribution to the theatre of the absurd; in another, it is a parody of the absurd itself. The young cockney seems always in greater danger of losing his mind than his life as he is set to simmer in an Irish stew of young tarts and old rebels, pimps, perverts and counterspies, religious crackpots and preposterous patriots. Of course he can make no sense of any of them (neither, at first, can an audience) except for

Teresa, an unspoiled skivvy, who out of love brings him cigarettes and beer and eventually herself. But not even love can save him; he is to lose more than his cockney heart.

There is almost palpable shock in a theatre when the young soldier is shot down; death surely is out of place in a bawdy romp like this – and yet, after the stomping and the shouting, the jigging and joking and singing, the taunting of audience and author and everyone else in sight, after farce and folly have driven all else out of mind but folly and farce, the comic mask is for a moment wrenched aside to afford a glimpse into an absurd and unthinkable dark where grin and grimace are one. But only for a moment. After a decent brief lament by Teresa, the corpse pops up (Instant Resurrection in Behan's canon) and, facing the audience ends the play with a song about the bells of hell.

The song, though this is not apparent from the text, is directed at the audience, and the audience has already been made to identify – at times almost physically – with the outrageously simple-hearted, perversely obtuse, people on stage. And the stage now becomes, as it was for Shaw, a pulpit for Behan; his preacher, a corpse that claps its hands and sings, gives chapter and verse for the dramatic shenanigans just concluded; the pseudo-heroic in Irish life has been deflated, political posturing – parochial or imperial – in a world that can 'muck about with the moon' is mocked as against all common sense and common humanity, and only the victim of this madness can in the end enter a plea of innocence.

The play is Brendan Behan's private effort at still another kind of *aggiornamento*.

Behan, a modest man, made some claim for the play's originality, a claim that may be allowed but with qualification. It was originally called 'An Giall', for he wrote it first in Irish (within, he says, twelve days) and saw it performed, without notable success, in Dublin's Damer Hall in 1957. It was not until Joan Littlewood's London production the following year that its success became spectacular and, in short time, international.

A frothy resemblance to 'The Threepenny Opera' – and to Gay's earlier opera – had been noted quickly enough, but a more striking similarity to Frank O'Connor's 'Guests of the Nation', and especially to Ian McKenzie's dramatisation of that short story, seems to have been passed over. As for the jokes, scattered like studs through the dialogue, Behan pilfered them with assurance from any source at hand – two of the best being lifted directly from 'Ulysses', whose author would have been delighted. Behan at times even plagiarised himself, a habit that in his later work becomes tiresome.

'Borstal Boy' in 1958 can be called, and it has been, Behan's Portrait of the Artist as a Young Delinquent. It is the most carefully written of all his work, and in the sense that it creates its own form it is also his most original. Ostensibly an autobiography, the story of his early years in jail, it has at the same time the quality and effect of a novel of adolescence: experience becomes knowledge, idealism becomes reality, boy becomes man. This particular boy, intelligent but ignorant, learns quickly.

Walton Jail in two months, he says, had made him very anxious for a truce with the British. He had concluded not only that everything he had read or heard in history about them was true, but that they were even crueller bastards than he had thought. He was defiant no longer but frightened of them.

This fear is the beginning of the boy's wisdom, and as wisdom grows, fear recedes, until at last he is brought to the realisation that human decency is a quality of persons, having little to do with politics or party or blood or belief, and that it can and does flourish even among his traditional enemies. It is this growing realisation that gives the book its shape.

An impressive amount of modern writing, whether or not in every case myth and experience are made co-ordinate, centres around a 'descent into hell' – a drop from one level of hopelessness to another until, in a writer like Beckett for example, the final drop is through language itself into despairing silence. Not so with Behan. He reverses the process and his book, as John Wain put it, 'spirals upwards, beginning at the very bottom of a pit of despair and ill-treatment and ending in the sunshine'. The figure is apt but not perhaps fully adequate.

There are no loose ends to 'Borstal Boy', nor is the reader left, in the end, up in the air. The book is calculate, complete, finished – a not always easy achievement, especially in the deceptively easy genre of autobiography. A more adequate figure may be that of *two* spirals which, like Yeats' interpenetrating gyres, create and sustain tension and form by the immergence of one cone of darkness into a second cone of light. Or to put it differently, the horror of the first part shades off into the humour of the second as imperceptibly as one colour changes into another in and out from the centre of a mechanical top that can be set spinning at the touch of a child's hand.

This is Behan's most engaging quality as a writer that, like a child at play, he takes such obvious and so highly communicable a joy in what he is doing. And like a child, the artist sets his own rules which have very little to do with other kinds of rules which may govern other kinds of worlds outside the bounds of the special game he is making up. Behan's world is that of the immediately given – sight, taste, touch, sound, smell – especially, in all its extravagant raciness and variety of rhythm and accent, the sound of the human voice. Excluded from this world are pronouncements of judgements, the posing of Big Questions, the probing of psyches – almost, one might say, thought itself, man's distinctive genius for destroying his own innocence and everybody else's happiness. Behan's innocence here in the company of queers, rapists and murderers, among torrential streams of criminal obscenity, under a constant rain of blasphemies indistinguishable for the most part from that piety that generates them, is untouched. He is at play, and it is the game so finely contrived that it appears essentially simple.

That is why it is beside the mark to compare, as some would, Behan to Genet. Behan was not a criminal by nature or inclination (he was not a prisoner by inclination either, but by political luck), and he would certainly have had no truck with *mystiques* of any kind, still less with those gravitating around a cult of the sinister or the depraved. His intent was not to confront but to accommodate. He was not interested in the criminal mind but in men who, by a luck no better than his own, had been judged to be criminals. And as a man he was himself profoundly, at times obstreperously, responsive to those who seemed to him not to have had a fair shake of the tree. These were the people he wrote about and this was his reason for writing, and as this kind of writer he is always able, often excellent, and never profound.

Unfortunately, Brendan Behan was not always this kind of writer. Four other books have been published, two of them posthumously, and a fifth and presumably final publication is reported to be on the way. None of these can add a whit to his reputation as a writer or much to his reputation as a wit.

'The Scarperer', published in 1964, is a novel, actually a novella, which Behan wrote for serialisation in the *Irish Times* as far back as 1953. It is a police romance on the model of Ewen Montague's 'The Man Who Never Was', but peopled with affable Dublin crooks and told now in an Irish brogue. Not as gripping as a Graham Greene 'entertainment', not quite as charming as the usual *divertissement*, it falls not too flatly between the two. That is about as much as can be said for it. And that is why it is painful, if you read the *New Statesman* or the blurb on the book's jacket, to be told that this 'without doubt is the most important book of its kind to be published this century.' Unless there is some cunning reservation hidden in that statement about

the book being *sui generis*, this is to force upon the wholly acceptable principle of *nil nisi bonum* a burden it cannot bear. Behan
himself, I think, would have been embarrassed by this kind of
well-meant but misplaced praise, for he as much as admitted what
he himself thought of 'The Scarperer' when he explained why he
wrote it under a phony name. (The pseudonym was Emmet
Street, the name of a road in North Dublin opposite that in which
he was reared.) He was, he said, 'short of the readies', and *Irish
Times* had then ninety fat pounds to ready and steady him.

His other three books – 'Brendan Behan's Island' (1962),
'Hold Your Hour and Have Another' (1963), 'Brendan Behan's
New York' (1964) – are for the most part catchalls of a newspaper
man (though there is a one-act play, 'The Big House', in one of
these books, and something very like a short story in another)
who, suddenly become famous, finds his old columns have taken
on an importance for others and a price for himself beyond any
former expectation, but not, happily for him, beyond immediate
realisation. As the quality of this work declines, the format of
each succeeding book seems to become fancier and more formidable – heavier paper, more copious illustration, generous
margins, larger print – as if openly to signify that these are
strictly publishing ventures, designed possibly for the gift trade,
for people who can own books without much feeling the need to
read them. Perhaps they are, but for all that they can be looked on
kindly, not critically, for from one to another we see in them a
finely talented man, witty and valiant still, but gone wearier and
wearier, going like a swimmer out from shore ever more weakly
into depths whose surfaces are less and less able to sustain him.
Brendan Behan of Dublin, writing in the first of these books of
the island he knew and the people he loved, was a man whose
rebelly ramshackle company was good and invigorating, and a
different man from the Brendan Behan writing in the last book of
a New York where he was a celebrated but transient immigrant
who, turned the wrong way out, chit-chatted along Broadway to
an off-beat tune he could seldom find the right words for.

The fifth and last book – to be called 'Confessions of an Irish
Rebel' – will not in any real sense be 'written' at all. It has been
talked into a tape recorder from which it has been passed out
through the typewriter of Mrs. Rae Jeffs of the staff of Behan's
British publisher, Hutchinson, to Bernard Geis Associates, the
New York publisher, who has promised duly to acknowledge –
but who will distinguish? – Mrs. Jeff's contribution to the Behan
canon.

A few days after Brendan Behan died, a mutual friend just

returned from Dublin stopped me in Sheridan Square to talk about the news from Ireland. Had I heard what were Behan's last words? I had not till then. As he lay dying, apparently in a coma, an attentive nun hovered about solicitously. As she bent over him a last time to smooth a pillow, Brendan opened one dark eye and whispered to her: 'Thank you, Sister – may you be the mother of a bishop!' 'The story is probably not true,' our friend said, 'but it could have been.'

Indeed it could have been. And that could almost serve as epitaph for Brendan Behan.

2

THAT OLD TRIANGLE

By Benedict Kiely

IN the end of all, the hostage, Leslie Williams, rose from the dead in full view of the audience and mocked the bells of hell that go ting-a-ling-a-ling, and in cheery parody of Saint Paul, asked the grave where was its victory, and death where was its sting-a-ling-a-ling. The victory and the sting are in the sore truth that the bold Brendan, quiet for the first time since he yelled as a newborn babe, has drawn the Glasnevin coverlet over his head and is no longer to be found raising the roof or entertaining the customers in any one of the many places of public resort that lie between the two White Horses: the one in Greenwich Village and the one that Michael O'Connell keeps on Burgh Quay by the River Liffey.

He was, as we say in Ireland, much missed at his own funeral, for he was always one to bury the dead with sympathy but with a spirit that mocked at mortality, and he would have appreciated the verbal slip that made one graveside speaker say that he had had the privilege of being interred with Brendan. He meant interned: and while the dead man in his time had had his reservations about the joys of internment he would, of a surety, have preferred them to the nox perpetua of the grave. Dying as a 'lark,' he often said, had no attractions for him. It was a lonely business and he was, even to the detriment of his work and health, the most gregarious of men. The one thing he found most wearisome in prison was to be locked in his cell. In 'Borstal Boy' he described how he sat in his cell and listened to the approaching noises of a key jangling and door banging. He hoped that the warders would at least open his door even if they had nothing better to give him than kicks and thumps. For to fight was to be in company and even that rough sort of company was better than solitude.

Even in prison, where he spent eight years of his short life, he did his best to beat off loneliness, and so much of the best of what he really wrote – not talked into a tape-recorder when he was sick – is that very odd thing, a shout of laughter from the cell. The name of the prison in North Dublin City where his play 'The Quare Fellow' was played out to its end in a hanging, was ironic enough to please him: Mountjoy, for yet further irony abbreviated into The Joy. An ale brewed in that part, his own part, of

Dublin was called by the same name as the prison, and an enticing advertisement displayed at one end of Russell Street where he was born, and visible every Sunday, said: 'Joy Be With You in the Morning.'

Song erupts from the punishment cells as the curtain rises on 'The Quare Fellow', a song that Behan adapted from a cruder original by another prisoner.

He understood and could make laughter out of the old lag's perverted pride in his record between stone walls and iron bars. One of his old prisoners boasted to a novice about his glorious hardships in Kilmainham where the novice had never had the privilege of doing fourteen days without a mattress and dining, as in the happy land far far away, three times a day, – except that there was nothing on the menu except skilly. And the patriotic blood of warder Regan boiled at the boasting of a prisoner who had been in English prisons; for the warder saw this boasting as a sign of the Irish national inferiority complex and wanted to know what better could you find in Dartmoor or Parkhurst than a good Irish-leather cat o' nine tails, or a warder's baton loaded with lead from Carrickmines.

Behan's temperament, a comical sight more than that of Lovelace, made light of prison, because prison was familiar to his rebel family and his Irish blood and, in prison as outside it, he had a passion for making mockery of authority. He looked, for instance, in 'Borstal Boy' at the Governor of Walton Prison, England, and saw nothing very much to be impressed by in this tweedy, desiccated old Englishman with some pretensions to horsiness and an inability to speak audibly. Yet Brendan saw with contempt how the screw, the prison officer and the chief warder listened to the mumblings of this effigy as if he was Jesus Christ or Plato or Dale Carnegie.

Dunlavin, the greatest of all his old lags – called, by the wild comic spirit that made Behan laugh even at those patriotic things that were dearest to him, by the name of a Wicklow village famed in the heroism of the Rebellion of 1798 – expresses his disgust at having to live cell-by-cell with a sex criminal. But those who are alive, even though they lie in jail, must accommodate themselves to the conditions of living, and Behan took his durance vile as a priceless part of his experience and all the time intended to use his prison memories when he turned to writing. Once when I complained to him that if things were as they once were the rising cost of living in Dublin would land me in jail for debt he said, with affected horror: 'Don't take from me the one advantage I have in this hard-backed book business.'

101

The Four Courts

His best hard-backed book, superbly done as the scattered dictated notebooks were not done, was, too, in the oddest way, a continuation of the considerable library written by Irishmen in English prisons or on the run from English law: Doheny, Davitt, Kickham, Tom Clarke, Darrell Figgis, et alia. Through his mother's brother, Peadar Cearnaigh, who wrote the song, by no means his best, that was to become the Irish national anthem Behan was very much part of all that. But no accused patriot adding to that holy scripture 'Speeches from the Dock' – a paper-backed national piety once a bestseller in Ireland – could have permitted himself the humour, the mockery, the bad language of Behan; and the resonant Carlylean voice of John Mitchell, of Young Ireland in 1848, orating rather than writing his classical 'Jail Journal', finds an uproarious reductio ad absurdum in 'Borstal Boy'.

The Joy, then, was a fine and quiet place compared with The Bog (the long-term Portlaoise Prison in the flat Irish Midlands) and had, because of a kindly governor whose copy of 'War and Peace' Behan borrowed and never returned, the name of being easy: easy, that is, until matters went as far as hanging. Then the laughter sourly dies in the cell and the prisoner called Neighbour tells how once for two bottles of stout he took the hood off the unfortunate man who had just been hanged, or topped, and how he wouldn't do it a second time not even for a bottle of whiskey, because of the sight he saw: the black face, the head twisted round, the eyes staring with the final fear.

Brendan was in the Joy, not for politics as was his wont, but, like the bold Thady Quill, for 'batin' the police', when the last man to be hanged in the Republic of Ireland went to the drop. With two warders he and the condemned man made a four for handball. He drank the condemned man's daily bottles of stout because the crime for which the unfortunate fellow was doomed to suffer had been done under the influence of that beverage and he could no longer be convinced that Guinness was good for him. When the pitiful wretch asked Brendan if hanging hurt, Brendan assured him with his own special type of kindness, that he didn't think so but then he had never been through it himself nor had he talked with anyone who had. He was in prison for politics when the original of the Quare Fellow was hanged; a pork-butcher who had murdered his brother and filleted the corpse so skilfully that nothing was ever found. It was one of Behan's more lurid jokes that the murderer had sold his brother as fresh pork to the Jesuit Fathers in Tullabeg. That Brendan Behan, like Lord Byron, woke up to find himself famous overnight, right in the middle of the English debate on capital punishment, was in no small measure due to that hanging; and that was the only good turn hanging ever did him or anybody else. For decent people are as interested in hangings nowadays as they were on the night before Larry was stretched – in public; and think of all the long years during which Tyburn was London's greatest theatrical draw, a popular open-air theatre.

The famous drunken appearance on B.B.C. television came to the aid of the hangman in the popularisation of Brendan Behan, and that was the only good turn drink ever did him. Now that I've raised the question, and since it must be answered, let me say how grossly by the lower-class London papers the drunken legend was exaggerated. It was no news at all that an Irishman should be sober and working. Yet while Brendan did not invite such publicity he did nothing by word or deed to squelch it: he went a long ways further than Samuel Johnson in believing that to be talked about, well or ill, drunk or sober, was the best way for a writer to bring in 'the Readies': meaning dollars and pounds. It is the way of the vile world, but Henry James, and others, would have demurred. It is customary and correct to lament the drinking and the waste, as my friends, Irving Wardle, the London critic, and Francis MacManus, the Dublin novelist, have done, but it is also a wonder that so much writing was done in such a short time, not because of the impediment of drink but because Brendan never had any regularly developed habits of work, and being, as I said, the most gregarious of men, he craved company, which in Dublin frequently leads to drink unless you care to join the Legion of Mary or the Pioneer Total Abstinence Association which neither he, myself, nor any of our friends in Dublin ever showed any fanatical signs of doing. The mornings I have been aroused at six or seven to find Brendan smiling at the foot of my bed with the bright idea that we could start the day well in the early bars in the fruit markets or on the docks! There's a sweet story that once when, following his first trade, he was painting a ceiling in the Land Commission office in Merrion Street, and had his head out the window for air and looking at the people, James Sleator, the painter, passed and invited him round the corner for a 'tincture', and Brendan went and never came back, leaving the ceiling half-painted and his kit for anyone who cared to collect it. He painted the flat of the poet Patrick Kavanagh, for free but, for laughs, did it, in the poet's absence, a complete and total sable. He had an odd sense of humour. He was also, we must remember, in his final years a sick man with a sickness that craved the sweet heat of drink and that the drink only aggravated.

He was, first and before all, a Dubliner from that restricted area of North Dublin City to which true Dubliners confine the high title of the Northside. The rest of the North City is suburbia inhabited by provincials. After that he was an Irishman and a member of the underground Irish Republican Army at its most troublesome period since the bloodshed and burning ceased in 1923. He was, by his own definition: 'a bad Catholic' or, as Irish euphemism has it a 'lapsed' or 'non-practising' Catholic.

His I.R.A. activities brought him at an absurdly early age to an English prison and a Borstal institution, gave him the makings of his best book, which either as autobiography or as part of the literature of penology has established itself as a classic, and inspired him for various reasons with a healthy respect and a liking for the English people. Although his first feeling, after two months studying and experiencing the brutalities of the warders in Walton Jail, was that he was most anxious for a truce with the British, that not only was everything he had ever read or heard about them in history true but that they were a lot worse in the way of bastardy and cruelty than he had ever reckoned they were. In a world of tyrants they seemed suddenly to him to be as tyrannical as any and his defiance was changed to fear. But later acquaintance with kindlier types – they included sadly enough a decent Borstal chap called Neville Heath later to be renowned, although Behan with splendid restraint does not say so nor fully name him, as the sadistic murderer of two women – made him modify his opinion, and he allows himself that deliberately exquisite understatement that the British were very nationalistic. He was, too, always glad and grateful that London Town gave him his first and best welcome as a playwright and that once when on the way through England from Ireland to France he was arrested under a deportation order the British authorities deported him not back to Ireland but onwards to France, paying his fare – a humorous and decent people.

For all previous sharp statements about the neighbours he made amends in the character of Leslie Williams, the hostage, also a voice from a prison, an ordinary young English boy caught fatally and wonderingly in a situation he cannot hope to understand, Teresa, that sweet young country girl, so lovably played by Celia Salkeld, an orphan as the hostage is, tells him that Monsewer, the old mad owner of the house in which he is held, is an English nobleman: 'he went to college with your king.'

SOLDIER (i.e. Leslie): We ain't got one.

TERESA: Maybe he's dead now, but you had one one time, didn't you?

105

SOLDIER: We got a duke now. He plays tiddly winks.

TERESA: Anyway, he (i.e. Monsewer) left your lot and came over here and fought for Ireland.

SOLDIER: Why, was somebody doing something to Ireland?

TERESA: Wasn't England, for hundreds of years?

SOLDIER: That was donkey's years ago. Everybody was doing something to someone in those days.

Caitlin Ni Houlihan and John Bull have never spoken so simply, so comically nor so wisely to each other as in that passage. And mad Monsewer was, indeed, English, the son of a bishop, and had gone to 'all the biggest colleges in England and slept in one room with the King of England's son' until one day because his mother was Irish he discovered he was an Irishman, or an Anglo-Irishman, which in Behan's misleading definition was 'a Protestant with a horse.' Anglo-Irishmen only work at 'riding horses, drinking whiskey and reading double-meaning books in Irish at Trinity College'. To become Irish, Monsewer took it 'easy at first, wore a kilt, played Gaelic football on Blackheath . . . took a correspondence course in the Irish language. And when the Rising took place he acted like a true Irish hero'. But when he lays down his bagpipes and raises his voice in song, as all Behan's people, including himself, were forever ready to do, his father's blood proves living and strong:

> *In our dreams we see old Harrow,*
> *And we hear the crow's loud caw*
> *At the flower show our big marrow*
> *Takes the prize from Evelyn Waugh.*
> *Cups of tea or some dry sherry,*
> *Vintage cars, these simple things,*
> *So let's drink up and be merry,*
> *Oh, the Captains and the Kings.*

Monsewer has a dual, lunatic significance: the house he owns and in which the young hostage is held and accidentally killed by his rescuers is, as Pat the caretaker says, a 'noble old house that had housed so many heroes' and is, in the end, 'turned into a knocking shop'. It is also romantic, idealistic Ireland fallen on sordid, materialistic days, and that a madman of that most romantic people, the English, should in his imagination, lead the last Irish Rebellion, playing the pipes and making heroines out of dacent whores, would seem to be a fair chapter of our national story. But the house is more than heroic Ireland down in the dumps; it is the world in a mess and God gone off his rocker: the very first stage direction says: 'the real owner isn't right in the head.' Monsewer, in fact, is one of Behan's visions of God, and as he parades, salutes, plays the pipes and sings of tea and toast and muffin rings, the old ladies with stern faces and the captains and the kings, he falls into line with images of the Divinity that appear elsewhere in the plays and prose.

The ministers of religion, because of Brendan's experience with prison chaplains who had to tell him that as a member of the I.R.A. he was excommunicated, seldom come well out of his story. Yet God is, nevertheless, not to be judged by the deficiencies of his servants; and Dunlavin, satirising the Higher Civil Servants talking big in the back snugs of pubs in Merrion Row, defends the Almighty against their patronisation: 'Educated drinking, you know. Even a bit of chat about God at an odd time, so as you'd think God was in another department, but not long off the Bog, and they was doing Him a good turn to be talking well about Him.' The same turn of phrase, almost, recurs in 'The Hostage' when Meg attacks the canting and quite impossible Mr. Mulleady. In a good cause Brendan was never afraid of repeating himself.

The cynical Meg may say that 'pound notes is the best religion in the world', even though the 'chokey bloke' in 'Borstal Boy' points out that some men are so miserably constituted that they would be incapable of being happy anywhere, even if they were in the Ritz Hotel with Rita Hayworth in the bed and a million pounds in the bank. God could sometimes be faltering, as Monsewer was, in his judgements of people, for Ratface, the altar server in prison looked like a true-blue sort of Englishman with a mind no wider than his backgarden, and capable of skinning a nigger if he got somebody else to hold him, and of sending the hide home to his mum. Yet Brendan reckoned that if Ratface was in the state of grace the Lord would be as well pleased with him as if he was St. Stanislaus Kostka, the saintly Polish boy. Ever since an aged faltering Jesuit had read out to the juvenile gurriers of the Russell Street area assembled for a retreat in the St. Francis Xavier Hall in Sherrard Street, the notes the Jesuit had intended for the Little Lord Fauntleroys in the Belvedere Preparatory School, Brendan had had an especially comic image of St. Stanislaus. Regardless, the Maker of All Things had compensatory qualities. Following in a mob the course of the Saviour's Passion around the Stations of the Cross in the prison chapel, the prisoners were enabled, in a passage that is pure Hogarth, to fuse and mingle and exchange cigarettes and even fragments of food. The crooked greyhound men taking the doped dog to the races in one of the best sketches in 'Brendan Behan's

Island' were respectfully pious enough to warn Brendan that it wasn't a lucky thing to mock religion and they going out to 'do a stroke'.

If the law that excommunicated the I.R.A. had not existed and Brendan had been allowed to go to confession he would have missed the sight of one of the nastiest of the warders slipping and falling and floundering in a snowdrift, and shaking his fists in anger and falling and floundering again while the prisoners from their cell windows roared with laughter. Brendan sat down again at his table and, in the terms of an old Gaelic proverb, thanked God and his Blessed Mother for all that. That proverb points out that God never closes one door but he opens another, or that if He taketh away with one hand He giveth with the other. Pressed down and flowing over, in fact; and we are back with God as Monsewer, a decent fellow, not quite in control of things. Whose actions even when He doesn't plan them too well frequently turn out for the best. Even the 'lapsed' Catholic comes out in defence of the Old Faith when he tells Hannen Swaffer, the columnist, who has just announced that he is a spiritualist, that Catholicism keeps a better type of ghost.

Borrowing a sentence from the lingo of his beloved Dublin streets, he was fond of saying that every cripple had his own way of walking. It is also true that every writer has his own way of writing, and I have already pointed out how wonderful it was that so much good writing came out of Brendan's gregariousness and chronic restlessness. His great kindly spirit had to express itself in every possible way, and what was writing – if it didn't go on too long – but another form of movement. 'Borstal Boy', 'The Quare Fellow', 'The Hostage' and the better portions of the notebooks or sketchbooks are the considerable achievement that he has left us, although one stage direction in 'The Hostage', reading, 'what happens next is not very clear', would seem to indicate that Behan threw his hat (he never wore one) at the whole business of writing and said: 'Joan Littlewood, the dacent girl, will look after that and – the Begrudgers.' Reading your own works, he argued in his sad book on New York, was a sort of mental incest but, as a rule, it is better at least to write them; and to the New Yorkers who have been disappointed in what he had to say about their stupendous city, which as cities go he loved next to Dublin, I keep saying that the book was not so much written as spoken by a sick and weary man into a tape recorder.

Yet even in the tired ramblings-on of a man who was so close to the grave, there is flash after flash of the spirit that made him the most entertaining companion I have known or am ever likely to know. One night in Michael O'Connell's White Horse when sick with laughter at his antics – (i) Toulouse-Lautrec, by walking up and down the floor on his knees, (ii) the Poor Old Woman, Mother Ireland, with the tail of his jacket over his head for a shawl, (iii) an aspiring Irish politician mouthing every platitude ever heard from an Irish platform and borrowing a few from the pulpit, (iv) Sex in the Abbey Theatre, for which there are no words but only mime and the mimic is now forever motionless – I remember thinking that if he ever got a wider audience he'd make a fortune. I can't claim much credit for the prophecy: it came easy. My sadness is that this great kind comic man held the stage only for such a brief time. We have left, as I say, the plays, including the one-act 'The Big House', effective on radio but a dead loss on the stage, the autobiography, and what was good in the notebooks. To come, there may be yet another piece of dictated autobiography, and the play 'Richard's Cork Leg' which, borrowing a title from a very irritated James Joyce, was to be the meeting of all Ireland around the grave of Honor Bright, an unfortunate whore done to death by gunshot on the Dublin mountains forty or so years ago. 'The Scarperer' we may dismiss, forgiving as well as we can the person who wrote the publisher's blurb to say that Behan having accomplished this and that, now turned to the novel and made it his own: the sort of praise that can only damage a writer's reputation. But for a delightful brotherly sidelight on the ways of the wonderful Behan family and on the lovable father and mother, Stephen and Kathleen, Dominic Behan's 'Teems of Times and Happy Returns' is valuable.

Brendan had a happy boyish belief that you could find a good man everywhere and, being a friendly man, he liked meeting people and being always, in some ways, a boy he liked talking about the important people he had met. He liked being invited to the inauguration of President Kennedy. Who, politics apart, wouldn't have? He liked talking about the late Gilbert Harding, who was a fine man, and about Oona Guinness, who is a great lady, and about John Betjeman who is, anyway, a sort of Irish institution. I detect an ironic flicker of the eyelids, even if by then they were very tired eyelids, when he would say – 'As Hemingway once remarked to a friend of mine.' He was vain and proud of his success and eternally talkative. But he was not so much a name-dropper as a friend naming friends, and Princess Margaret and Rosie Redmond, the Dublin whore, were all equally to him just people.

Rosie Redmond we will remember from Sean O'Casey's 'The Plough and the Stars', and I feel that Brendan and certainly his father, Stephen, knew stories about her that even O'Casey had not heard. This is not the place to tell them, yet the mention of her fair name brings me by a most 'commodius vicus or recirculation back to Howth Castle and Environs', to the 'fort of the Dane, garrison of the Saxon, Augustan capital of a Gaelic nation', to the city built around the body of the fallen Finegan and the more catastrophically fallen giant: Haveth Childers Everywhere.

A city, he said was a place where you were least likely to get 'a bite of a wild sheep', and the test of a city was the ease with which you could see and talk to other people, and New York was the friendliest city he knew. But Dublin was his own town, not the middleclass Dublin that John Mitchell had found a city of bellowing slaves and genteel Dastards, and that Pearse said had to atone in blood for the guilt of Robert Emmet's execution, but the Dublin of the fighting poor who were led by Larkin in 1913 and the Dublin with the everlasting memory of the Post Office in flames.

It was the Dublin, too, that the prisoners, Neighbour and Dunlavin, fondly dream over in 'The Quare Fellow'. Meena La Bloom belonged to it, who, with Dunlavin's help, gave many's the Mickey Finn to a sailor; and May Oblong who debagged the Irish M.P. on his way to Westminster to vote for Home Rule, and locked him in her room, and neither for the love of her country or his would liberate him until he slipped a fiver under the door; and the patriotic plumber of Dolphin's Barn that swore to let his hair grow until Ireland was free; and Lottie L'Estrange that got had up for pushing the soldier into Spencer Dock. They belong in Joyce's Nighttown and on the shadowy streets that Liam O'Flaherty wrote about in 'The Informer'.

Behan's Dublin, too, as the plays show, was as much or more that of Boucicault and the Queen's Theatre Variety as it was of the Abbey Theatre, except when O'Casey was in possession of the Abbey Stage. And his Dublin was my Dublin from 1937 onwards, and with brotherliness he once told me that I was one of the few country — he knew who had enough in him to make a Dublin jackeen. From an early age he had what he called a 'pathological horror' of country people, because to a Dublin child the symbols and exercisers of authority, teachers and civic guards, all came from the country, the provinces, and the jungle began where the Dublin tram tracks came to an end. But his heart was too big for one city to contain, and it opened out to Ireland, the Aran Islands, London, Paris, New York; although to the end he had his reservations about Toronto and Berlin – as they had about him.

He would have died and almost did die for Ireland, but he was sharply conscious of the delirium of the brave in the Robert Emmet pose of the dying hero. It was fine to feel like Cuchullain guarding the Gap of Ulster, his enemies ringed round him, his back supported by a tree, calling on the ancient gods to support him until the last of his blood was shed. But if the only spectators were two Walton jailers, Mr. Whitbread and Mr. Holmes, clearly Private Compton and Private Carr in later life, and if Mr. Holmes was methodically beating you up, then the hot glow went out of the heroism. You could be mangled in an English prison and who in England would give a damn about you. At home you might afterwards be revered as a martyr and a lot of use that would be if you had already gone through the mangling. He was brave from boyhood to death, but there were no false heroics about him and he felt that between mangling and martyrdom there should be some satisfactory, poetic and preferably unpainful relationship.

Like Peter Wanderwide – and how Behan would have mocked at me for quoting Belloc – he had Ireland 'in his dubious eyes'. In Irish and English its ballads and classical folksongs were ready to his lips, and when he wasn't deliberately roaring his head off he could sing. At penal work, digging on the Borstal farm, his fork uncovered from English soil a golden apple still hard and tasty, and biting it surreptitiously and feeling the juice sharp on his tongue he thought of Blind Raftery, the poet, and of the spring coming, after the feast of Brigid, to the wide plains of Mayo. But in the swift switch of humour that was characteristic of him he would admit that digging was an activity he wouldn't pick for pleasure and would tell how his father, Stephen, during a Dublin strike brought him out to help farm an acre of land on ground, at Glasnevin, once associated with Dean Swift. Stephen dug for a bit with great unction, talked about the land, how his ancestors came from it, how healthy it was, and how if they kept at the digging they might uncover relics of Swift or Vanessa or Stella or Mr. Delaney. But next day, bored, he got a countryman to dig the plot in exchange for Stephen doing the countryman's strike picket-duty. That is a touching, endearing picture of father and son – two rare comedians.

But Brendan was grateful for the golden apple and the good weather. He was always grateful and pious in good weather, and the day he found the apple was the sort of day that made you aware that Christ had died for you. A bloody good job, he thought, that he was born in rainy Ireland and not in the South of France or Miami Beach where he'd have been so grateful and holy for the sunshine that Saint Paul of the Cross would have only been trotting after him.

As a great swimmer, next to the sunshine he loved the sea: the eastern sea at the Forty Foot, the swimming pool famed in 'Ulysses': the laughter of the western Galway sea which, according to Louis MacNeice, juggled with spars and bones irresponsibly. Brendan did not view it so sombrely. On the Aran Islands, and along the Connemara shore, and in Glenties in Donegal with the Boyles and the Harveys, he claimed he could forget all the cruel things of this world. He wrote so pleasantly of the night, after the licensed hours, in the pub in Ballyferriter in Kerry, in the Southwest, when the Civic Guards obligingly sent word that they were going to raid so that the customers could withdraw a little up the mountain slope, taking supplies with them, and drink in peace until the raid was over. He described in one of his best pieces of prose a night of starlight on some of the most impressive mountains of Ireland, he sitting with some of the local farmers, talking Irish and drinking his pint, and proudly conscious that he was sitting on a lower slope of Mount Brandon.

That was a happy Irishman at home in Ireland. Mount Brandon, as he said with proprietary pride, was called after his patron saint, Brendan the Navigator, who, the legend says, reached the New World before either Norsemen or Columbus and who left to all who came after him the promise of the Isle of the Blest that all mariners might one day find.

3

THE RAW AND THE HONEST

I

A CRITICAL LOOK
By Kevin Casey

THE Liffey is a lazy river, turf-brown and sullen; it flows slowly through Dublin as if well aware of the futility of a journey which must always end in the Irish Sea. It has managed to capture the imaginations of artists and writers but one can not help feeling that it is left cynically unmoved. Down it comes from a pool in the mountains, indifferent to Joyce, indifferent to Gogarty, indifferent to the lament and, above all, to the swans.

It succeeds, however, in fulfilling a number of important functions. Not least amongst these is the division of Dublin city into two sections, a division as defined as those made by the Thames or Seine and occasionally as dramatic as the Berlin Wall. It was in Eccles Street, north of the Liffey, that Mr. Leapold Bloom lived with Molly and ate, with relish, the inner organs of beasts and fowls but the real Joyce country lies south of the river, temporarily ballasted by the perilous respectability of office incomes, riding lessons and last mass.

The North side is generally regarded as being the home of the 'genuine' Dubliner. It is old and decaying and many of its houses are at present undergoing Corporation demolition. Some streets look like multiple stage-sets; house roofs and gables have been taken away, lunatic stairs lead upwards and then stop abruptly, door frames stand without the advantage of surrounding walls and untouched houses are like single teeth in an ancient gummy smile.

In tenement life, money and privacy are almost invariably in short supply. Families are divided by thin plaster walls; communication with the neighbours can be achieved by a raised voice or a thump on the ceiling; people with radically different views and personalities are thrust close together to share a common present and a parallel past. It would be naïve to think that there is anything very attractive about this way of life but it is true to say that day to day semi-communal living must often border and sometimes tangle with the essential stuff of drama. Sean O'Casey discovered this and was accused by his early

113

Abbey critics of photographic realism. They ignored his genius for preceptive but heightened character drawing and speech and were apparently irritated rather than impressed by the blending of comedy with tragedy, melodrama with farce which, though new in the theatre, could hardly have been strange in the tenements where jocosity was often the only alternative to the depths of depression. His early plays, like the legendary fruit-cakes of innumerable grandmothers, were made up of a little bit of this and a little drop of that, a rich but by no means haphazard mixture directed towards the release of the listeners' emotions. In his autobiographies he tells of the influence that the great melodramatist Dion Boucicault had on his work, how the cry of despair and the deep belly-laugh were always more vital and exciting than the patient whimper or the refined chuckle. His characters are seldom if ever inhibited by the conventional belief that emotions should be carefully kept to oneself but his genius allowed him to create a person like Juno who, while saying and feeling things that would be ludicrous in any Sandymount parlour embodies, at the same time, a truly heroic, tragic dignity.

Brendan Behan lived on the North side of Dublin at a time when tenement life as O'Casey knew it, was gradually being obliterated. But the characteristics of generations can not be pulled down as easily as houses and even after his family had moved to Crumlin, he must have felt the influence of Russell Street, diluted perhaps but ever present, in ways of talking, ways of acting, ways of thinking. One of these characteristics – probably indeed, the most potent and understandable – is the grouping of all society into 'we' and 'they'. 'They' represent what is, figuratively speaking, the other side of the river. 'They' feel superior and must, in consequence, be brought down to size. The balloons of their egos must be needled and burst. They must be laughed at and recognised as imposters. This is really a form of self-protection and, as such, can be an eminently healthy and rewarding pastime. And if a touch of malice is added to the humour every now and then, the end, a well-deserved deflation, can still be argued to justify the means. It can also have a more serious purpose. It exposes the villain as well as the petty hypocrite, the evil as well as the pompous; it can spotlight injustice and often helps correct it for there is nothing quite so undermining as derisive laughter. This combination of constructive and destructive humour is, I believe, the supreme driving force in the writings of Brendan Behan.

Life isn't, of course, a matter of black and white. There are innumerable shades of grey. We are not engaged in a massively

114

organised game of Cowboys and Indians. But the essence of the theatre is not that it be imitative of life. It is, rather, that life be invested with and enriched by the power and the vitality of the dramatic imagination. The great writer is the man whose imaginative vision is, in itself, great.

Brendan Behan was not a great writer. That he might have been is interesting though arbitary speculation. But he was a very good one. He had an extraordinarily agile sense of humour developed along the lines which I have mentioned. He had a real appreciation of the value and colour of words and a gift for their use in a heightened dialogue which, at its best, was almost as good as O'Casey's. He had a compassionate understanding of human suffering and what John Jordon, in a perceptive phrase, has described as 'an almost Dickensian flair for the humorously macabre element in a situation'. (1)

His major work was 'Borstal Boy', a highly individual autobiography. It describes his experiences of Borstal and prison life and is undoubtedly one of the finest books ever written on these themes. He wrote two plays for the theatre, 'The Quare Fellow' and 'The Hostage' and two radio plays, 'The Big House' and 'Moving House'. Before gaining international recognition he contributed a large number of articles to various newspapers and magazines. Some of these have been collected in a book called 'Hold Your Hour and Have Another'. His publishers have also issued two books, 'Brendan Behan's Island' and 'Brendan Behan's New York' which were tape-recorded by a well-meaning but misguided member of their staff. It is unreasonable to expect that anybody's casual conversation will make good reading and, entertaining though they are in parts, it would have been better if these rambling and untidy books had never been issued.

II

'Borstal Boy' was first published in 1958. It is an astonishing book, filled with a vividly bizarre collection of characters: Flash Harry Lewis and Lovely Ball, Chewlips and Shaggy and Callan, patriot and overcoat robber who, while the prisoners were exercising in the yard, could imitate, without being detected, the scream of a war-pipes and as frustrated warders fumed and fretted, everybody marched to the stirring strains of 'O'Donnell Abu!' The same Callan gave vent to his political feelings at odd moments during the day. 'Uuuuu- uuu- uup the Rep – uuuub – lic, Beeee- haaaan!'

The book opens as Brendan Behan is being arrested in a

Liverpool digs. He isn't unduly disappointed to be leaving an establishment where the landlady's sister, despite big, buck teeth, prays every night for the protection of her person and modesty and the other lodger hopes that he might be given the strength to partake sparingly of all refreshments, even innocent ones like tea, lemonade, herb-beer, ginger-pop and cocoa.

Taken to the C.I.D. headquarters in Lime Street, he prepares a statement which, he feels certain, will stir many a heart when printed in the Irish newspapers; unfortunately the first hearing is held in camera and he doesn't get an opportunity to read it. He talks to everybody and is grudgingly liked by most. He matches remark with remark but preserves a kind of innocence that is capable of being surprised when a man with the name of O' Sullivan turns out to be highly unsympathetic to his ideals or when an Inspector refers insultingly to Roger Casement. But he quickly realises the 'justice' of it. 'He could do that here; and we could abuse the old Famine Queen at home, or the Black and Tans; and every man to it in his own country. And then to come over here and plant bombs in it, you couldn't expect them to love people for that.'(2) He is sent to Walton Gaol, makes friends and observes apparent enemies.

But even as he is observing and laughing, mocking and learning, the serious inner-man is active also:

'I was glad that even in this well-washed smelly English hell-hole of old Victorian cruelty, I had the Faith to fall back on. Every Sunday and holiday, I would be at one with hundreds of millions of Catholics, at the sacrifice of the Mass, to worship the God of our ancestors, and pray to Our Lady, the delight of the Gael, the consolation of mankind, the mother of God and of man, the pride of poets and artists, Dante, Villon, Eoghan Ruadh O'Sullivan, in warmer, more humourous parts of the world than this nineteenth century English lavatory, in Florence, in France, in Kerry, where the arbutus grows and the fuchsia glows on the dusty hedge in the soft light of the summer evening.'

He has an argument with the prison chaplin on the part played by the Church in Irish politics and is beaten up by the warders for his trouble. Sore all over, sick and clammy, his mouth raw and bleeding, alone in his cell, he has a thought that is typical of both the man and the book;

'It's a queer world, God knows, but the best we have to be going on with.'

When the long-delayed Assizes come around the unsuspecting judge asks him if he has anything to say and he is at last given an opportunity to deliver his highly verbose speech from the dock. Sentenced to three years in a Borstal he shouts 'Up the Republic' and feels that he has joined the company of heroes until, outside the door of his cell, a wardress who is accompanying a young, weeping girl, launches an attack on him:

"'Dry your tears dear and 'ave a look at the 'ero. 'Ere's a poor girl got in trouble, and is up over doing away with 'er baby, though, of course, it will only mean she'll be bound over", she put in quickly, "and you young pup 'ave nothing better to do than coming over 'ere making trouble for everyone and your poor Dad and Mum worried to death, I'm sure, over in Ireland, and, you young pup, give you three years Borstal, did he? I know what I'd have done, tan your backside for you, that's what I'd have done, taken down your pants and given you a good tanning and sent you back on the boat tonight. And this poor girl 'ere –" She glared at me and I didn't know what to say to the old bitch, only wished the screws would open the cell and let me get to hell away from here.'

The Governor of Hollesley Bay Borstal is a kind and intelligent man. Brendan Behan likes him. He also likes Mr. Davis, his housemaster and most of the other Borstal Boys and is fortunate enough to discover a warder whose father comes from Mayo. He is made a member of the painter's work party and wins an essay prize which is presented to him by Colonel Craven, a local landowner, who, it is reputed, 'Took his perishing clothes off and shaved off 's moustache time the Titanic went down, and pinched a woman's nightdress. When they shouted "women and children first" 'e comes runnin', wearin' a shift, carryin' a bundle and screamin "Save my little babby". When they'd landed safe and sound they discovered it was two bottles of Scotch wrapped up in a face towel.' At a sports, the highlight of which is a cross-country race, he encounters a character who has little of the rebelliousness but all of the independence of Alan Sillitoe's famous runner.

'What happens but the bloody forger is in that (the race) and the long forger's legs of him and his beaky counterfeit nose brought him before anyone else, also due to the conservation of his energies behind the incinerators, where he slyly hid and rested himself while the other poor honest bastards – well, by comparison poor simple robbers and rapers and murderers – went round the second time.'

The rest of the book is crammed with incidents and characters, sharply described, sharply drawn, all a little larger than life, all throbbing with a humorous vitality that is unique in contemporary writing. The dialogue too is always good.

'"He'd be a good man and you in chokey all right", said I, "and Galsworthy. When I was in Walton I got a bloody great book of his, 'The Forsyth Saga'. When I was starving with hunger and perished with cold in the old flowery dell all alone, it was like having a feed of plum pudding and port wine."

'"Did you know", said Joe, "there's a book called 'Crime and Punishment' – it's about a geezer that kills an 'ore with an 'atchet."

'"It's by a Russian called Dostoyevsky," said I. "Did you read it?"'

'"No," said Joe, "can't say as I did. But I 'eard a bloke tell it once. You know the way you tell a film. It was double good. But the best book I ever saw in the nick was the Bible. When I was in Brixton on remand, I 'ad one in the flowery. Smashing thin paper for rolling dog-ends in. I must have smoked my way through the Book of Genesis before I went to the court."'

Finally, he is brought to the Governor's office, given a notice of expulsion from Britain and released. On the following morning he stands on the deck of a boat as it sails into Dun Laoghaire harbour. Everything is as remembered; the mountains, the spires, the Pigeon House, the road along the edge of the bay – all the old familiar landmarks. He hands his expulsion order to an immigration officer who welcomes him home.

'"It must be wonderful to be free."

'"It must," said I, walked down the gangway past a detective and got on the train for Dublin."'

This brief synopsis can only give a faint indication of the worth of 'Borstal Boy'. It is a rebel's book, a rebellion against pettiness. It contains no trace of bitterness though the author can be devastatingly critical when he chooses. There is nothing intrinsically funny about prison life but the strength of Brendan Behan's personality colours everything as he notes, with a delighted laugh, the unusual, the unexpected, the bizarre. Beneath much of the fun there are serious humanitarian undertones, pleas for tolerance and understanding. The book has been accused of unnecessary coarseness but prisons don't resemble Novitiates or preparatory schools for the daughters of gentlemen and surely honesty is a finer and more admirable quality than caution.

We are moved, shocked and entertained but the over-all effect of 'Borstal Boy' is a surprising one based, ultimately, on the force of contrasts. Brendan Behan reading, in the noisy prison, a novel by Mrs. Gaskell seems as incongruous as Macheath in Brecht's 'Threepenny Opera' leaving the Wapping whores, placing a pair of steel-rimmed spectacles on his nose and carefully checking the books of his remarkable business. But the breadth of the author's sympathies leads us to recognise that when the 'we' and 'they' split in society passes the personality game stage – to become, say, racialism or any of the other intolerances of our time – it is usually based on the major incongruity of mutual ignorance. There can be no doubt about the direction of Brendan Behan's first loyalties but he seems to have had an unfailing understanding of multiple points of view. By using this understanding with such power and truth he achieved a great deal.

III

In 'The Quare Fellow', a maximum amount of bizarre comedy is extracted from a hauntingly tragic situation. In 'The Hostage' a maximum amount of farce is loaded into a situation which, under the strain, collapses into something that is neither comic nor tragic. Although 'The Quare Fellow' is entirely devoid of the machinery which is generally thought to be essential for dramatic construction, it does move, with a strong degree of inevitability, towards its climax. One feels, however, that if some director had decided to bring into the cast of 'The Hostage' a young lady whose talents were entirely restricted to the production of innumerable doves from the same coloured handkerchief, she would have been in no way out of place and nobody would have been less worried than the author. Of Joan Littlewood, Brendan Behan wrote ...' ... (she) ... suited my requirements exactly. She has the same views on the theatre that I have, which is that the music hall is the thing to aim at for to amuse people and any time they get bored, divert them with a song or a dance.' (3) He certainly couldn't have had these views when he wrote 'The Quare Fellow' and the chances are that they were more Miss Littlewood's than his own. They represent, of course, a perfectly valid approach to the theatre but if variety is to be the object of the exercise, it should be balanced by some degree of conventional discipline. Control, in 'The Hostage' is hidden in the wings: irrelevancy is the key-note of the proceedings and the piece, although theatrically effective within its own limitations, is by no means as good as 'The Quare Fellow'.

The opening exchanges in 'The Quare Fellow' make it immediately obvious that this prison play is a far cry from the shadowed worlds of Sartre or Genet. A warder comes on, puts cards in the doors of two vacant cells, opens the others, shouts loud abuse at a prisoner who is singing the by now famous ballad of 'The Old Triangle' and leaves. One by one the prisoners come out of their cells. The first is an old lag, the second a gentle and easy going man.

PRISONER A: Nice day for the races.

PRISONER B: Don't think I can make it today. Too much to do in the office. Did you hear that commotion last night, round in D wing? A reprieve must have come through.

PRISONER A: Aye, but there's two for a haircut and shave. I wonder which one's been chucked?(4)

Two executions have been planned but now only one is to take place. Dunlavin, an old man who has spent most of his life inside, is the local source of information for his cell contains the water-pipe joints and he can pick up the steady morse-code of news which is tapped out from all over the prison. He is busy getting his cell ready for a visit from an official of the Department of Justice called 'Holy' Healey – a process that consists, mainly, in the vigourous polishing of a large enamel chamber pot and the pinning of innumerable holy pictures on the wall – but takes time off to tell what he knows.

DUNLAVIN: Just a minute till I put back me little bit of china and I'll return and tell all. Now which quare fellow do you mean? The fellow beat his wife to death with the silver-topped cane that was a presentation to him from the Combined Staffs, Excess and Refunds branch of the late Great Southern Railways was reprieved; why him rather than the other fellow is more nor I can tell.

PRISONER A: Well I suppose they looked at it, he only killed her and left it at that. He didn't cut the corpse up afterwards with a butcher's knife.

DUNLAVIN: Yes, and then of course the other fellow used a meat chopper. Real bog-man act. Nearly as bad as a shot-gun or getting the weed-killer mixed up in the stirabout. But a man with a silver-topped cane, that's a man that's above meat-choppers whichever way you look at it. (5)'

They see, from one of the cards on the vacant cell doors, that 'Silvertop' will soon be joining them to start his life sentence. From the other card they learn that a 'sex-mechanic' will be coming also and Dunlavin is extremely indignant at the company he is forced to keep. The conversation comes around to the man who will be hanged on the following morning and Brendan Behan manages to inject considerable horror into the descriptions of what is to be expected; the long wait in the death cell, the embarrassed tension of the warder, the doctor with his back turned to the fatal trap-door. But we are still made to laugh:

DUNLAVIN: ... Do you know who feels it worse going out to be topped?

PRISONER A: Corkmen and Northerners ... they've such bloody hard necks. (6)'

After two young prisoners, who have no really important function in the play, drift in and out, Warder Regan and 'Silver-top' enter. Regan is a strange and complex character who is used, one suspects, as a spokesman for Brendan Behan's opinions on capital punishment and the society which allows it. Not entirely convincing – ideological mouthpieces seldom are – he does provide a strong balance to the nervous indifference of almost everyone else. 'Silvertop' is quiet and withdrawn; the unexpected reprieve is far more terrifying to him than the long expected death sentence. The 'sex-mechanic' on the other hand has a great deal to say and is appalled at the thought of having to fraternise with murderers whom, he believes, would be justified in taking their own lives. There is a large amount of comic thrust and parry as the two young prisoners, who have drifted in again, watch, through a window, some of the inmates of the women's prison and Dunlavin and Neighbour, a bent old man who hobbles around with the aid of a stick, reminisce on May Oblong, Lottie L'Estrange, Lady Limerick and the many other formidable ladies of the town whom they have known in their day. Some of the prisoners leave for medical inspection while in a scene that is very much O'Casey, Dunlavin and Neighbour, both of whom claim to suffer from rheumatism, are rubbed with methylated spirits by Warder Regan.

WARDER REGAN: Raise the leg of your trousers. Which leg is it?

DUNLAVIN: The left, sir.

WARDER REGAN: That's the right leg you're showing me.

DUNLAVIN: That's what I was saying, sir. The left is worst one day and the right is bad the next. To be on the safe side you'd have to do the two of them. It's only the mercy of God I'm not a centipede, sir, with the weather that's in it. (7)

As Regan bends and rubs, Dunlavin, complimenting him on the healing touch of his hands, drinks deeply and secretly from the bottle, much to the disgust of Neighbour who is afraid that there will be none left over for himself. 'Holy' Healey, a character direct from almost any of the Whitehall farces, then makes an appearance. He is chiefly of interest as a foil to Regan who is determined that nothing will be allowed to gloss over the legalised brutality of what is to come.

Healey gives a holy picture and some unctuous advice to Silvertop who, as the act ends, attempts, with splendid dramatic

121

irony, to hang himself in his cell.

Up to this point, the tragic undertones of the play are almost concealed by the rough surface of comedy. In the second act, which is set in the prison yard during the evening of the same day they become more obvious. Nervous indifference now swells into real expectancy. Each life is presented so that it seems to have, as an important focal point, the hanging which is to take place on the following morning. The characters, although never completely individualised, are distinctly recognisable and, as the play gathers pace, we realise that the first act was really nothing but an overblown exposition scene.

The prisoners examine a half dug grave and joke about it; but veiled in the comedy is a note of slightly hysterical tautness. Laughter is now being used to cover fear. A new character, Prisoner C, a young man from a Western island is introduced. A surprisingly sentimental creation, he represents one of the few consistent themes to be found in Brendan Behan's writing – innocence resisting the forces of corruption. By a singular but acceptable coincidence, a new warder, Crimmin, comes from the same island and their relationship provides a slender secondary theme. Neighbour, having laid his Sunday bacon against the chances of a reprieve coming through for The Quare Fellow, remembers him with great bitterness.

NEIGHBOUR: ... I saw the quare fellow in here a couple of years ago. He was a young hard chaw like you in all the pride of his strength and impudence. He was kicking a ball over in A yard and I was walking around with poor old Mockridge, neither of us minding no one. All of a sudden I gets such a wallop on the head it knocks the legs from under me and very nigh cuts off my ear. 'You headed that well', says he, and I deaf for three days after it! Who's got the best of it now, young as he is and strong as he is? How will his own ear feel tomorrow morning with the washer under it and whose legs will be the weakest when the trap goes down and he's slung into the pit? And what use is the young heart? (8)

This is an important speech for it provides us with one of the two pictures that we are given of 'The Quare Fellow' and his youth and vigour seem to make his fate all the more tragic. The other picture is given by Prisoner C:

'I don't believe he is a bad man. When I was on remand he used to walk around with me at the exercise every day and he was sad, when I told him about my brother, who died in the Yank's army and my father, who was buried in the demolition of Manchester . . . He was great company for me who knew no one, only jackeens would be making game of me, and I'm sorry for him' (9).

Four prisoners are detailed to complete the digging of the grave and Crimmin learns that he is to assist Regan at the execution. Donnelly, a warder who, up to now, has been presented as a brash loud-mouth, is seen talking with buttering banality to the Chief Warder and we are not at all surprised to learn later that he is playing a game of prison politics and hoping for promotion. The scene ends with a strong conversation between Regan and Crimmin and the arrival of the hangman, another farcical character, who inspects, through a grill, the thickness of 'The Quare Fellow's' neck so that he can make accurate calculations and do a clean job that will avoid strangulation or actual decapitation. Crimmin is unable to disguise his revulsion at all this but Regan points out that: 'Himself has no more to do with it than you or I or the people that pay us, and that's every man or woman that pays taxes or votes in elections. If they don't like it they needn't have it.' (10)

This is a pivotal point that forces us to participate and commit ourselves to an opinion, for or against capital punishment. The act has been punctuated by comedy – especially notable are the efforts of an English prisoner to have someone contact a friend of his so that bail can be arranged – but the real emphasis has now shifted to the strata of tragedy. A man will soon die and his death has, as Regan points out, at least our tacit approval. We are as involved as the on-stage characters; their embarrassment, hostility and pity must be ours also.

The first scene in the third act takes place later that night. Donnelly plays his treacherous politics and the Prison-Governor, wearing evening-dress, confirms that there will be no reprieve. (It's an ill and ironic wind – Neighbour will have a double ration of bacon on Sunday morning.) Regan talks to the Chief Warder and, as in the case of Holy Healey, allows no artificial or righteous gloss.

Society is indicted; murder, whether it be legalised or not, must corrupt. The scene ends on a note that must surely be the most savagely and grotesquely funny in contemporary drama. Jenkinson, the hangman's assistant, plays a concertina and sings a hymn as his boss completes his gruesome calculations.

JENKINSON: (sings)

> My brother, sit and think,
> While yet some time is left to thee,
> Kneel to thy God who from thee does not shrink,
> And lay thy sins on Him who died for thee.

HANGMAN: Take a fourteen stone man as a basis and giving him a drop of eight foot . . . .

JENKINSON:

> *Men shrink from thee but not I,*
> *Come close to me, I love my erring son,*
> *My blood can cleanse thy sins of blackest dye,*
> *I understand if thou canst only weep.*

HANGMAN: Every half-stone lighter would require a two-inch longer drop, so for weight thirteen and a half stone – drop eight feet two inches and for weight thirteen stone – drop eight feet four inches. (10)

And so on, appallingly funny until we realise, with guilt, that Christianity – even the odd brand which Jenkinson represents – is based on charity, mercy and compassion but the face of society is held together and kept clean by a justice that is a rigorous as the old eye for an eye code; a justice inextricably mixed with vengeance. The last scene in the play takes place on the following morning. Two warders are on-stage. An unseen prisoner shouts about the execution as if it were a race, in a style made famous by a well-known Irish sports commentator. The hour strikes. The warders bless themselves. 'The Quare Fellow' is dead. Crimmin is carried across the stage – he has fainted – but the atmosphere of the prison is suddenly animated by what must be relief. Loudly Neighbour claims his winnings. Loudly, the English prisoner worries about his bail.

'The Quare Fellow' is a play about Capital Punishment, about people reacting to it, to each other and to enforced conformity. It is not a psychological study, nor does it depend – as Koestler's famous 'Reflections on Hanging' do – on polemics. Its effectiveness is almost completely theatrical, probing and blending emotions, hammering home effects. It reminds one of a wake; keening mixed with dancing, laughter with tears. Written in dialogue that is always precisely suited to situation, it is an important contribution to world theatre.

There is little point in giving a detailed description of 'The Hostage'. Its line of action is not vital and its scenes, with a few obvious exceptions, are almost interchangeable. It is set in a Dublin lodging-house owned by a likeable fanatic called Monsewer (shades, already, of music-hall and Eddie Gray) who is unaware that 'The Troubles' are over. So busy is he blowing discordant blasts on a war-pipes that he is also apparently unaware that his house is being conducted as a brothel by the caretaker, Pat, a one-legged, highly-talkative, ex-I.R.A. man. Pat

124

thinks very little of the new I.R.A. who are causing trouble at the Border. 'This is nineteen fifty nine and the days of the heroes is over', he says, but Meg Dillon, his mistress, is delighted to hear that Monsewer has given them the use of the house. 'Where the hell were you in nineteen sixteen when the real fighting was going on?' he asks her. 'I wasn't born', she replies. This would appear to be the new Ireland – but there is a lot to come yet. An I.R.A. man is awaiting execution in Belfast prison and, in reprisal, a young English soldier is captured as he is coming out of a dance and brought across the border. He eventually arrives, under guard, at the brothel. Buoyantly bewildered by what is going on, he makes friends with Teresa, a young orphan who is employed there as a maid. (Like Prisoner C in 'The Quare Fellow' she represents innocence resisting corruption). There is then a considerable amount of slapstick, principally provided by the ladies of the house, two homosexuals called Princess Grace and Rio Rita, a farcical social worker named, in the best Ben Travers tradition, Miss Gilchrist and Mr. Mulleady with whom she prays but who is actually a secret policeman in disguise. What's going to happen to the hostage? is the only question posed and, typically enough, it is resolved without difficulty at the end when, in a police raid he is accidentally killed.

At first glance, all this may seem to be thin enough material. Closer examination confirms the validity of this impression. Brendan Behan expanded 'The Quare Fellow' from an early radio script, 'The Twisting of Another Rope'. It was, we know, tightened in production by Miss Littlewood but the changes were minor and the script closely resembles the one used by Alan Simpson when giving it its world première at the Pike Theatre. 'The Hostage' was originally a short and rather sentimental play, written in Gaelic. Obviously, a mass of new material was added and one can't help suspecting that more than a fair share of it was brought about by Miss Littlewood and her players, operating in theatre-workshop conditions. It bears the marks of this; an impromptu air, an ad-lib atmosphere, a bit of crack for the cast. Perhaps Brendan Behan was trying to make some other points. That soldiers seldom know what they are fighting for? This, after a thousand and one fat American novels hardly seems worth saying. That the I.R.A. didn't know what they were fighting for? That when we achieved freedom we didn't know what to do with it? More interesting but unlikely. One could go on for pages but the exercise is facile. It seems that a modern music hall atmosphere was, indeed, the aim of the play.

On this level, it is good. Thin on the page it has, on the stage, a wild energy, a gusto, a colour and a number of exceptionally funny songs that make it more entertaining than many a well-tailored play bearing the hall-marks of impeccable craftmanship. But one can not help feeling nostalgic for the raw, honest power of 'The Quare Fellow.'

IV

A third play, 'Richard's Cork Leg', on which Brendan Behan was working for some time before his death, was never completed. Set in a graveyard it is, by all accounts, nearer in treatment to 'The Hostage' than 'The Quare Fellow' and probably wouldn't have marked any considerable advance. We are now being threatened with 'Confessions of an Irish Rebel', another tape-recorded book which will almost certainly have all the faults and the few merits of previous similar experiments.

Two plays and an autobiography – not a large body of work. Yet quantity, in this instance, is not an important measure and the quality of what we have is impressively high. Brendan Behan had generous talents and he used them generously. A little too generously, perhaps, and too often in the wrong places but if he hadn't the man wouldn't have been the man and we would all have been the poorer for it. What future generations will think of his work remains to be seen. At the very least, one knows, with certainty and gratitude, that the Irish theatre can never be quite the same again.

SOURCES

I

(1) Chapter on the Irish Theatre in 'Contemporary Theatre' Stratford-Upon-Avon Studies No. 4. (Edward Arnold Ltd. 1962.)

II

(2) Borstal Boy by Brendan Behan. (Hutchinson 1958) All quotations in this section taken from edition published by Transworld Publishers Ltd. in 1961.

III

(3) Brendan Behan's Island—an Irish Sketch-book. (Hutchinson 1962)

(4)	The Quare Fellow by Brendan Behan (Methuen 1956)	Act One.
(5)	"	Act One.
(6)	"	Act One.
(7)	"	Act One.
(8)	"	Act Two.
(9)	"	Act Two.
(10)	"	Act Three, Scene One.

MEET THE QUARE FELLA

Fred O'Donovan who directed the film 'Meet The Quare Fella' talks to Ken Stewart

KEN STEWART: How did 'Meet the Quare Fella' come to be made in the first place? Whose idea was it originally?

FRED O'DONOVAN: Well, it all happened in a public house . . . where most creative ideas come from. One evening I was having a quiet drink with Eamonn Andrews and we were discussing possible television shows and films. The thought had occurred to me that if we could get people like Frank O'Connor, Sean O'Casey and Brendan Behan to do interviews, this would be of great value to the literary world, and, needless to say, would be first-class entertainment. So we immediately decided to start with Brendan.

KEN: Was it that you thought of him as the most challenging subject to begin the series?

FRED: Yes, we thought of him as the most difficult subject. We felt we would have no problem with Sean O'Casey and that Frank O'Connor would collaborate.

KEN: Had Brendan ever mentioned literary spoken word recordings by other writers in conversation with you? Did he ever even jokingly express the desire to undertake something of the kind – either filmed or recorded – in the future?

FRED: No. In actual fact, at that stage in my life I didn't know Brendan. I knew him as a person in show business would know another person who is an entertainer and supplies entertainment to the public. But I didn't know him as a person. To be quite honest, I hadn't the respect for Brendan that I had after we worked together. I felt that Brendan was quite a good writer who was certainly an exhibitionist.

When he first arrived at my office and we started talking, my first reaction was to catch him and throw him down the stairs. But by the time we finished our little film I was one of his greatest fans. I really believe this man had a great feeling, a brilliant brain. Although he was self-educated – he had no formal education after 14 – he could talk brilliantly about most of the great writers and painters. His French was first-class. His Irish . . . well, I believe it was first-class, and his English I don't need to elaborate on.

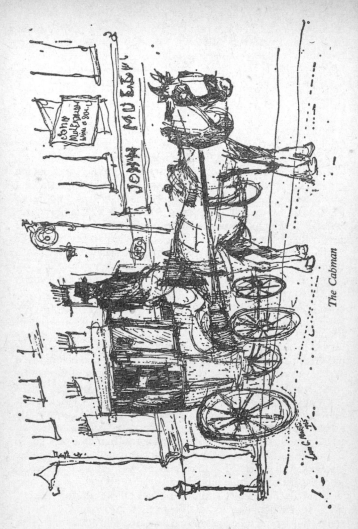

The Cabman

KEN: I remember he once told me how pained he was when writers wrote about him disparagingly without having first met him. He practically pleaded that people should come along to talk with him before they put a word on paper. Did he mention this to you?

FRED: He did, indeed. As a matter of fact, we got very friendly because Brendan first lived on the North side of Dublin, not far from where I first lived. We knew the background of this side of Dublin, so we were on familiar ground.

I found that if I had written about Brendan Behan at any stage in my life before I met him, it would have been a completely shallow, false, superficial account. Whereas the Brendan Behan I came to know was, to my mind, a very different man to the image he projected.

KEN: Would you agree that a great many accounts of him are grossly inaccurate or merely superficial – that not nearly enough personal research went into many interviews?

FRED: Yes, I think so. These were often the result of very short meetings with him. And, of course, you have numerous American writers who are prepared to write a thesis at the drop of a hat on somebody they've only just met.

I don't want to assume the mantle of one who can speak with authority on him; I think his close relatives and friends are the ones to do that – many people have come to me and asked for copies of the film we did. I recall in particular one Norweigian and one Swedish chap.

Now, I find this not very objective. To me, if you haven't met the man and he's only dead a year or two, and you want to write a thesis on him . . . well, it's hard to understand.

To me, Brendan Behan was a sad loss to Ireland because I really believe he hadn't written his best works. I also believe that in his innocence he was a fall guy for the literary world.

KEN: Just as Dylan Thomas was?

FRED: Exactly. When Dylan Thomas died the literary world needed another colourful character. They found Brendan Behan and they encouraged him. He was a sick man, he had diabetes. The drink he took would probably make him sicker, and as you know, in the interview he discussed this matter with us.

All the encouragement to drink many of his so-called friends gave him didn't help his life. And this is why I say I think he was a fall guy for the literary world.

KEN: Well, getting back to the beginning, will you give me the details of how the idea became a film.

FRED: Having conceived the idea I decided I'd have to pursue it. I then went after Brendan. Needless to say, it took quite a time to pin him down. We signed a contract and agreed on a date. Of course, it was just as difficult to get Eamonn Andrews as it was Brendan Behan. I had to set a date that suited both people. We allowed three days for the filming but shortly before we began I was informed by Eamonn that he couldn't give me three days.

But we went ahead as planned, anyway. I negotiated a deal with Louis Elliman who came in as producer with us. We decided to move in to Ardmore Studios on a Friday morning. I remember this very well.

About a week before our film Brendan was appearing in Ardmore on a programme of Ed Murrow's 'The Small World' which was a catastrophe. And I believe he made himself unpopular with the Ardmore staff.

So when they heard Brendan was arriving on the scene the following Friday morning they told me that if there were any problems they would be most un-cooperative. I assured them that Brendan would give no trouble whatsoever. I was rather edgy. I knew I was dependant on the crew. I felt that maybe I was asking for trouble.

KEN: Did you make Brendan aware of the crew's sensitivity?

FRED: I did, yes. I discussed this with Brendan and pointed out that I could easily have trouble on my hands if he didn't behave, and he said, 'Have no worries, Fred. As far as I'm concerned I'll say nothing, I won't even mention the other programme.

However, he walked into the studio on the Friday and the first thing he did was shout out to the crew: 'It's a small world, isn't it!' Which indeed endeared him to them. From then on we couldn't go wrong.

KEN: Were any special preparations made in the days preceding shooting?

FRED: We got Brendan on the night before the film and asked him to stay out in the Royal Hotel in Bray, where Eamonn, Lorcan Bourke and myself were going to stay so that we could keep him with us. We wanted to check over all the facts and generally review things. However, like all these sessions it turned into a political argument with Eamonn and Lorcan on one side and Brendan and myself on the other. We were arguing about emigration until about three or four in the morning.

When it finished we decided to go to bed because we had an early call in for seven o'clock, as we wanted to start shooting at eight. But something made me waken at six. I decided to get up and I went down . . . and there I found the bould Brendan sitting in the bar imbibing! So we had breakfast together – what breakfast he wanted to eat – and we went up to the studio.

We arrived at eight o'clock and organised to start at half-past eight. I had decided I would use a television technique of filming in which we would use three cameras running and at no time would we stop.

KEN: Along the same lines as Electronovision?

130

FRED: Exactly. You couldn't get any more than four minutes film in any one of the cameras. Which meant while two cameras were running I had to have one changed and re-loaded. It was very, very difficult, but we had some very good cameramen. We decided we'd take the risk because if it meant stopping every four minutes this would destroy the interview.

So we went ahead, and I must say it was magnificent to see and hear Brendan and Eamonn talking. Brendan did a wonderful job – he really couldn't have done better. We were out and back in our snug in the Royal Hotel by ten o'clock. We had an hour's film in the can. And this despite the fact that we had been told we would be days and days with Brendan. He went in there and I've never met anybody more professional.

KEN: What was foremost on his mind when he emerged from Ardmore?

FRED: He was completely satisfied and relieved. It was hard work and he was asked many searching questions.

KEN: Was it entirely impromptu or had he some idea of Eamonn's questions?

FRED: He knew nothing. He wasn't told any questions whatsoever. He had no preparation. He gave some wonderful answers. I'll always remember to my dying day some of the things he said. His particular little piece when Eamonn asked what he would like to have said about him in fifty years' time. His answer, which was very quick, was that he had celebrated his 87th birthday!

There was another remark that he passed which I think a lot of people should take notice of, and that was the one about the bombs and wars and suchlike. He was asked was he a warlike man because of the bombings and things he was associated with in the I.R.A.

His answer was: 'I'm not a warlike man. As a matter of fact, I was a highly ineffectual one. The Republican Army had sufficient good military sense never to make me any more than a messenger boy.'

Then he said something that I think is worth repeating. 'But what can anybody hope to do with bombs. I mean, why are the I.R.A. and the F.L.N. in Algeria and people of that sort the only ones to be sorted out. Other people use bombs, the Russians, the Americans the Germans. If you bomb Hamburg, Hiroshima, with huge, big bombs, it seems to be accepted as just historical necessity, so to speak.

'But I'm sure the Americans could find an excuse for dropping a bomb on Moscow and I'm sure the Russians could find an excuse for dropping a huge bomb on New York.

'But there seems to be snobbery about them. Why are the Irish, or even a section of the Irish, the only ones who are not permitted to use these little things. Is it because they use little bombs and the others use big ones?'

To me, this was a very profound statement. It showed a different Brendan Behan to the one that was known to the public.

When I look at this film now I can't help feeling terribly sad that his life was cut short at such an early age, because most really good Irish writers didn't write anything until they were over 40. Brendan hadn't even reached the stage of maturity where he could turn out the material we expected of him. I think Brendan would have turned out something marvellous if he had been given the time alloted to most people.

In the interview, Eamonn asked him: 'Do you fear death or don't you care?' He said: 'I do care. I don't like it. I don't like the dying lark at all. I don't think anybody does. I can give you instances of very eminent men surrounding themselves with all sorts of quacks, all sorts of doctors, surgeons and scientists, in an effort to stop in this world just a little while longer. A fellow said, "We know where we are, but we're not quite sure where we're going".'

KEN: When you got the idea of making 'Meet the Quare Fellow', did you experience an awareness – even, perhaps, subconsciously – that Brendan might not have long to live – that you had to make the film as soon as possible?

FRED: Well, it certainly wasn't conscious. Subconsciously, I may have. I had a list of twelve people, and since I made it six of them are dead. And that's only a few years ago.

One of them was a very young man, so I couldn't have subconsciously thought this was going to happen. But with Brendan maybe this was the case. My belief at the time was that I felt that the image of Brendan Behan that was projected by himself was not the true image. I knew that Brendan had a healthy respect for Eamonn and Eamonn had a healthy respect for him. I felt I was putting two people together who could speak honestly. They were very fond of each other and I knew that from these two people I would get honest questions and honest answers.

KEN: What was the reaction to the film?

FRED: It was quite fantastic. When it was transmitted on the B.B.C., we had letters from all over the place. They told us how wonderful it was to see Brendan Behan – if this was the real Brendan Behan we're proud of him.

KEN: It must have been a complete revelation to most viewers.

FRED: I suppose it was. Too many people were ashamed of him

because of the publicity and the fact that he was drunk on television. But they didn't realise that here was a man of great talents. They hadn't seen his plays, they hadn't read any of his material. All they knew was that he was a drunken Irishman.

And suddenly they see this man who projects a very intelligent, clever, witty image . . . a very human man. They realised that the position could be reversed and it could be Brendan Behan interviewing Eamonn Andrews.

KEN: Perhaps Brendan was saving the profound side of his nature for his old age and it was drawn out prematurely during the film.

FRED: Maybe this was it. It wasn't intended that our film should be now accepted as a sort of historic piece, but if we had done nothing else I'm glad we projected the true image, in my opinion, of Brendan Behan.

KEN: How widely was it shown?

FRED: It was shown in most parts of the world. Even at this stage we have more inquiries for it.

KEN: Did you ever think of it in terms of winning awards?

FRED: No, I really didn't. It's the last thing I think about in any endeavour. If you start preparing a film to win an award all you get is a technically beautiful film, and it can have no soul at all if you're not careful.

The only thought behind this was that I wanted to show a true picture of Brendan Behan. The techniques we used at that time were new. I used a lot of close camera technique. I never intended this film for the cinema, but when the powers that be saw it they said it would make a great cinema film. I objected because I knew a lot of the techniques I had used were not cinema techniques. I mean, when you use closeups in a cinema they can look ludicrous.

It was first shown at the Metropole in Dublin and had the longest run of any short for years. I attended it on a number of occasions and found people applauded and they laughed. I think for the first time it brought Brendan Behan to the average Dubliner. They realised that Brendan was one of them, that he was part of the country.

KEN: Did it strike you as curious that such a film profile had not been attempted previously?

FRED: Not really. His life was still young. It's like President Kennedy. There's a lot of material of him on tape and film, for which we're grateful, but nobody would have set out to make a film with the idea that he was going to die in a year's time. He was, in fact, one of the people on my list. One thought one had plenty of time. You never think of a young person dying.

KEN: To me, one of the most engaging aspects of the film was Brendan singing 'The Old Triangle'. How did that come about?

FRED: Well, this was rather funny. When we had finished filming I had warned the cameramen to keep the cameras running. I asked them to keep going after I told Brendan we were finished. So when Eamonn ended the interview, I told Brendan we were through. I asked him to do me a favour and sing 'The Old Triangle'. So he sat back, closed his eyes, and it was absolutely wonderful. He was completely happy; he didn't know the cameras were running. And it wasn't until he saw the film that he knew!

KEN: Would you say he took his singing seriously? After all, he had a large repertoire. Did it mean a lot to him?

FRED: No. I don't think so. I think he did it because he liked doing it. I don't think he was too serious. He didn't make many recordings. His brother, Dominic, recorded more extensively. I may be wrong, but I don't think he was particularly interested in that end of it.

The thing I felt about Brendan was that he was too busy living to write. Like all writers, when you're hungry you write well, but the moment fame comes you have to discipline yourself.

I think this is what happened to Brendan. Fame came quickly to him and he started to live – and live well.

KEN: Did he discuss future work with you?

FRED: At that time, he mentioned he was doing a book called 'The Catacombs' and a play possibly, 'Richard's Cork Leg'. We both admired O'Casey. We discussed the possibility of him deviating from writing about Dublin. He felt strongly that he shouldn't do this, as Dublin was his meat. I agreed with him.

KEN: Do you think he was over-criticised by his fellow Irishmen when he went abroad and behaved rather colourfully? Wasn't it somewhat unfair that he was looked on as a sort of ambassador when maybe all he wanted to be was a private citizen?

FRED: Yes. I think this was placing a big responsibility on his shoulders – a responsibility he didn't want. After all, there are many Irishmen who go abroad and get drunk and nobody knows anything about it. But because he happened to be a writer and had a certain amount of fame, it was different. And he did something that many of his fellow Irishmen have never done and would like to do: he was drunk on television!

You and I can quietly go into a pub and get drunk and nobody knows. But when you sit on television and get drunk there are millions of people looking at you. Well, of course this is what built up that image. As he said himself, he lives on one street and all the neighbours may be getting drunk, but nobody bothers. Yet he goes out and gets drunk and everybody knows about it.

KEN: One of his most significant remarks in 'Meet the Quare Fella' is that people should only be famous for a month.

FRED: This is terribly true. I think he realised that fame was stifling his work. The people visiting him, bringing him out for drinks, all the people who wanted to know him, to talk to him, the autograph hunters . . . and so on. You'd need 48 hours every day to live with this sort of thing. I wondered when he went to New York if he was going to try to get away from it all for a while, but you just can't.

KEN: What do you consider to be his greatest single achievement?

FRED: His first play, 'The Quare Fellow'. He wrote it at a time when the abolition of the death penalty was very much in the air and I think the play contributed to its abolition in Ireland certainly. We haven't had anybody executed since around that time. I think his play brought the realisation of this terrible thing home to the average person. It was an exciting play.

KEN: Do you think Brendan might have eventually appeared in films as an actor?

FRED: I think he would have made a great comedian after working with him. He had a wonderful sense of timing, a brilliant wit. I don't think he could have been disciplined as an actor. I don't think he would have wanted to be an actor. But after we made 'Meet the Quare Fella' he said that, as far as he was concerned, he could have gone on for four or five hours.

KEN: How many times did he see the film?

FRED: He told me he went in once without people knowing. He never discussed how many times he saw it, though. He mentioned that he felt a bit odd at times looking at it, but I suppose everybody does. It's more personal on television, but in a cinema – where you can hear the reaction around you – it can be embarrassing.

KEN: Finally, what is your strongest memory of Brendan?

FRED: He was a terribly sincere person who had very strong feelings and views. He hated hypocrisy. He hated sham. As he said himself, his audience wasn't the middle classes; his audience was his material. And I emphasise at this stage that I am not an authority on Brendan Behan. It's just a little excerpt of his life that I was associated with. I'm glad that I knew the man through this little film.

THE BROADCASTER

by Francis MacManus

I REMEMBER Brendan Behan in the morning, as it were, of his writing life when the dew was still on him. He used to ramble in to see me in old Radio Eireann in the very late 'forties and early 'fifties with scripts of short stories and talks and once with a few pages of a play about a man who was condemned to death for boiling his brother. Mostly he was alone. Sometimes he had his half-brother with him or some boozing friend he had picked up in a cattle market pub before any of us were awake. Alone or in company, he let the whole place know with a hullabaloo that he had arrived. With his gap-toothed grin and his fat round-cheeked country-woman's face he looked utterly harmless, like an overblown cherub.

The uproar was part of the Behan game. He could be docile as any lamb and sober as any judge when we got down to the job of reading and discussing whatever screed he pulled in a ball out of his pocket. But there was always preliminaries – an anecdote or two with appropriate jack-acting, a reminiscence of his time in gaol or in France, where he joined the Foreign Legion a few times for a bed and a meal, only to opt out the next morning; or even a song.

Once he arrived with a dreadful looking web-like gash on his chest oozing blood behind the remnants of a belly-open shirt. On his way into town he had passed over Leeson Street bridge and, seeing a few youngsters cavorting in the canal, he had peeled off his clothes and dived in to cool off; an old rusty broken bucket had met his chest. It took a lot of shouting and argument before he would let me apply an antiseptic. On another occasion he barrelled in with his mop of hair shiny and stiff like a gorgon's wig of hissing angry snakes. What had happened was that on his way down Granby Row – Matt Talbot country – he had found a man varnishing a door, demanded to see his union card, discovered he had none, lumped him in with Matt as a non-union man and tossed the can of varnish up in the air for the sake of the solidarity of the workers.

What goes up must come down. It came down on Behan's own head. By the time he reached my office the varnish had stiffened and he was nearly weak with hilarity. He called it Matt Talbot's revenge.

Hilarity often enveloped him in a gale. Friends were greeted with fusillades of perfectly amicable four-letter words. Girls of every age and shape were kissed. Once in his more rotund days I saw him pretending to buss a very stout, good humoured lady. Their equators prevented conjunction. 'The spirit is willing,' he shouted, 'but the flesh is in the way.' He knew that she knew that he was playing the Behan Game. She was part of the conspiracy, a member of the cast.

Meaningless expletives were only part of the game. They had nothing to do with Brendan Behan the writer who, to use Coleridge's distinction, had an abundance of genius and very little talent. Talent is what puts the scaffolding up and the cement on the bricks. It's genius that conceives the building to send it soaring.

And Behan, as I flatter myself for having perceived so early, had genius as a writer. In 1953 I told an English class in the University of New York that an Irish writer they must look out for, as a genius, was Brendan Behan. If I were as lucky with horses I'd be a millionaire but then how many horses have been like him?

Amongst other things, he did two short stories for Radio Eireann that were full of the genius and of the newness and freshness of it, as close to the truth as pain to a wound, full of Dublin gurrier speech, transformed by feeling and rhythm and vision into poetry, and shaped with the roundness of the much told tale. I think they may be read in his book about Ireland. Maybe he had told and re-told them. On paper they were alive. Over the microphone in his halting speech and strong accent, they were authentic with a life that had never been revealed before, except for a laugh. He could have been a great short story writer, speaking for a Dublin Joyce knew only by nocturnal adventure or guesswork.

But the craft was too lonesome for him. From beginning to end it meant quietness, solitude, working alone to discipline without an audience. I'll never forget how lost and alone he looked one day when, on receiving the red light signal in the studio, he failed to go ahead. When I went in to see what was wrong, he lifted his head, shaggy and jowled like the head of a battered Roman emperor and stammered, 'I'm not feeling too good. I can't let you down.' He was falling into a sort of mild coma. It was a warning of that disease which at last helped to carry him off. And remembering how it had carried off my own father as a young man, I nearly wept for him as for a doomed brother.

He was like a doomed brother a few weeks before he died

when he came into Radio Eireann to see the Productions Director, Micheál Ó hAodha, and myself. Both of us felt that he was making his last rounds and that he was conscious it was the last. He sat in an old armchair and for nearly an hour told us a story about an adventure he had had in New York. In his good days he would have told that story in a few minutes, a gale of words, with mimicry, gestures, splurges of good-natured abuse and obscenity, but here at the last he took a slow hour, groping in long silences for the words, the memories, that seemed to elude him down ever-receding caverns. Several times we tried to help him by suggesting words to him and every time something of the old fire flashed up, the old volcano erupted. 'Don't be putting words into my mouth,' he raged. 'Who's telling this story?'

He always told his story in his own way, precisely in his own way, and that was his genius. In his own way he wanted to give rather than to take. Did he die too young? Who can say? Perhaps he felt that he had given what he had been created to give.

Beannacht Dé len a anam.

PART THREE

Behanisms

Behanism . . . a word coined to combine atmosphere and personal relations . . . a word with a
certain degree of permanance . . . a word that
brings together The Catacombs, the drinking
houses, a car salesman with a rosary bead trick,
a man who almost swung a bottle in anger, and
the theatre. The world of Brendan Behan . . .
Behanism.

McDaid's

1

THE CATACOMBS

By Anthony Buller

THERE are unique intersections of time, place and people which enrich the sensibility with enduring and significant experience. Atmosphere and human relations are woven into shifting but coherent patterns and for a brief moment there is an ironic sense of permanence. In Dublin, one intense focus of this kind came into obscure but splendid being for a short time around 1950. It is remembered as *The Catacombs* and Brendan Behan was a vital part of its dynamic.

In the Dublin of the 'fifties it was an apt thought to compare the life of the city's beatniks with the underground and secret refuge of the early Christians. Each was a sect condemned by the Establishment; each was commanded to conform or suffer and each driven by necessity to create its own environment withdrew to an exclusive isolation. The comparison may be thin and almost irreverent but the preservation of truth and a faith in the distinction of each human soul, linked the Fitzwilliam Street cellars to Rome across the centuries.

The home of *The Catacombs* was partly in the basement of a large Georgian house and partly in a wooden structure at the back of the building and the presiding Peter was a London night club manager who came to Dublin during the war. The stone-flagged kitchens, the pantries and the cold passages in which he lived recalled the wealthy past owners whose servants had cooked and decanted and existed amongst them. Agitated spring-mounted bells attached by long wires to various parts of the upper storeys made them jump like puppets when called to carry coal or answer doors.

The new tenant was a happy, liberal man who was often in financial difficulties until he had the idea of converting his mouldering damp warren into a vast dormitory and a shelter for intellectual revelry. Physically *The Catacombs* had little to recommend it. There were beds everywhere; in the passages as well as the rooms. A plaster mucus oozed from most of the walls and the air was nauseant with the sweet smell of decaying mortar.

Yet it was here that Brendan Behan became intimately associated with sculptors and writers and others who were not beatniks in the strict sense; it was here he hitched his talented wagon to the stars of literary Dublin.

How or why the place became an intellectual catalyst it is very difficult to define but it is enough to look at some of the people and some of the things it shaped. Brendan Behan himself was one and it is worth remembering how often he announced he would write a play about *The Catacombs*. John Ryan, the Dublin artist and patron, whose creative and financial penicillins so often purify the aesthetic blood of the city, was a visitor and 'Envoy' his avant-garde magazine was partly gestated in *The Catacombs*.

Anthony Cronin was another whose personality was exposed to the abrasive atmosphere and he has captured a little of it in his novel 'The Life of Riley'. And, of course, there was the 'Ginger Man' with J. P. Donleavy or Mick as he was known then, watching and dissecting his subject for the book to come. Planning ahead to his theatre-to-be was Alan Simpson, unaware that the roaring, glass-waving Brendan across the floor was germinating two world-stopping plays.

The city was ripe for *The Catacombs* when it came into life. Almost the only city in Europe free of rationing and regulation it attracted foreigners – and the distinction in Ireland must be made – Americans. Nourished by the G.I. Bill of Rights the Americans were determined to invent the image of Bohemian Europe in Dublin when they found it did not exist. *The Catacombs* married to this urge the impatient inclinations of some Irish writers and artists. A number of I.R.A. men fresh from long years of disciplined imprisonment with ears, throats and nerves eager to compensate for deprivations and monotony were a small but important addition to the situation.

McDaid's public house in Harry Street also had an important part in all this and it was there that the informal initiations and the half-conscious process of selecting refugees for *The Catacombs* took place. If a man or a woman had a truth or a task that would not dissolve in alcohol or talk, it was a passport. Not that anyone thought in pretentious terms of this kind. It was all a matter of constructed accident and manipulated chance.

When the legal blessing of the state was withdrawn from public drinking the men of McDaid's – and the women – would gather their grey bags of clinking porter, their naked and more ostentatious bottles of wine and drift along night-polished streets to *The Catacombs*. Sometimes it would require the formal invitation of the presiding Peter himself although this was generally considered to be a repeating decimal. Sometimes there might be twenty and often fifty to join in the catacumbal pleasures.

The Catacombs generated no scandals and no sensations. The worst that might happen was a drunken woman's half-hearted attempt at a strip tease and this was rare enough. There was drinking and talking and singing with Brendan spinning a web of laughter and noise all around him.

But some sparks flew and some creative bonfires ignited. Perhaps one of the most extraordinary features of *The Catacombs* was Mick Donleavy's ability to read books in the whirling ideas and noise that spun, splashed and vanished down the drain pipe of alcoholic oblivion.

Sometime around three or four o'clock in the morning as the last bottles emptied those who could would stagger out into the cool freshness of a Dublin daybreak. Brendan had a flat in Mount Street – one room in fact – and this was convenient for himself and his friends when the rent was up to date. When it wasn't the lock of the room had to be picked with a piece of wire and this was a problem in the early hours of the dawn with shaking hands and swaying awkwardness.

It has been said that *The Catacombs* attracted lesbians and homosexuals and this is true in the same way that it attracted atheists and Christians. Their physical and theological inclinations were irrelevant to the place and however liberal its outlook it was not designed for exotic sexual appetites. What it gave was of far greater importance – an intellectualism diluted with a zest for laughter, living and people.

At times in Dublin you will be told in a confidential whisper that Brendan was a homosexual and some of this gossip dates from the days of *The Catacombs*. All the evidence is completely against this suggestion. He was outrageous in speech and spared nothing in order to shock and startle. For instance at a Salvation Army meeting he was guilty of an irreverence which can only be repeated in the very emasculated form: 'Up Hell and down with Heaven.' In the same way he made references to homosexualism which were interpreted more seriously at a later period in order to make a little splash in a puddle of scandal. This, at least, is the assertion of many close friends. As one said to me: 'There's many a woman would laugh to hear that said about Brendan.'

The presiding Peter of *The Catacombs* was not disinterested in organising parties and it has been said that he made a modest if steady income from the sale of empty bottles left by the guests.

It was not unknown for him to organise two or three parties on the one night which didn't allow the customers for his beds a lot of sleep.

But the talk was good and the drink was good.

Then, inevitably, *The Catacombs* began to decline. It became over-popular, a band wagon, and something of its quality died. It may have been exhaustion or its moment of truth might have ended and before it perished ignominiously the only begetter was no more.

Now *The Catacombs* is a jig-saw memory with the pieces scattered all over the world. Men looking out across the Hudson, the Seine, the Thames and above all the Liffey still pause as jets of memory fountain in their minds. Odours, songs, tastes and recollections crowd for a moment until the present sweeps in again and covers them like a wave on a seashore. . . .

2

HIS DUBLIN HAUNTS

By Terry O'Sullivan

In the obituary notice that I wrote for the *Evening Press* I said that Brendan Behan always frightened me. He outraged every one of the ten shades of meaning of the word 'respectable', and as I had been brought up on a road, not in a street, and forbidden to play with other little boys (because they were not respectable), the roaring entry of Brendan into my company always made my skin crawl. He was, in terms of decibels, a literary lion, and he knew it and roared all the louder because he had almost no teeth, and he was much happier in the pubs where his bellowing vulgarity would be listened to than in the lounge bars where bitchy epigrams are expected.

I'd say that Brendan was happiest in the White Horse, the nearest pub to the *Irish Press* group of newspapers, for, upstairs there, the 'Boss' O'Connell who owns the place, has an almost Franciscan gift of charming the birds. In Brendan's case, the 'Boss' O'Connell's almost miraculous power came through in a manner that would have driven a Balance and Control radio or television engineer mad. For while Brendan was sending out about 200 watts of 'ar thaobh na gréine, cois Sliabh na mBan', there would come the quiet soft Limerick interjection from the 'Boss'. 'Take it easy now, Brindan'.

I shall remember forever (because of my apalling respectability), the night that I walked into the White Horse, into Brendan's arms, into his beery embrace, into the smell of his sweaty shirt and the rasp of his unshaven cheeks, into the ear-bursting bellow of his voice as he raved like a dog at the moon . . . and then the stage whisper like an aside in some opera bouffe, 'Lend me half a crown.' I did, of course, for he frightened me.

Brendan Behan died owing me five shillings. But I can never repay Brendan Behan. The other half-crown he borrowed from me while we were accidentally together on the Aran Islands. I was in the Parish Priest's house, in solemn conclave when Brendan knocked on the door for he had heard I was on the island . . . and we ended up drinking ink-flat pints of Guinness dipped out of enamel buckets. The stout was awful, and Brendan's accent (for we were all speaking Irish), was awful too. But the man's vocabulary was fantastic, as he carried on a fluent conversation with the lantern jawed Aran men who, when confronted with the incredible, are as inscrutable as Arabs.

I believe now that had fate so arranged it, Brendan Behan would and could have spoken splendid French or German or Italian . . . but in an incorruptible Dublin accent.

Sooner or later there will come to Dublin the inevitable United States youngsters from young universities who (now that Joyce is written out for theses), will do something like 'A comparative study of Dylan Thomas and Brendan Behan.' That will make a crop of Doctorates in English, great gas (to use a Behanism) for Brendan and indeed such of his peers as Dylan Thomas.

The potential B.Phil (Oxon), or Doctor of Literature, (Little Rock), will risk cirrhosis of the liver, for much research has to be done through the medium of alcohol. Behan let the first bellow out of him in Gill's pub on the corner of Russell Street and the North Circular Road. The pub is also remarkable in that it is the nearest pub to Croke Park, but otherwise it is just another pub and you'll be disappointed if you are looking for atmosphere or for a built-in customer ready to remember Brendan for you. The boyhood of Behan was spent hereabouts, and even as I write the demolition of the old, dusty, dangerous houses, all about 150 years old, continues. The pub where he managed his first pint has now been 'modernised', and as so many of the locals have been moved out to the outskirts of the city (a theme developed by Brendan and his brother, Dominic), you'll find Behan's first pub a dead loss.

Better jump now to that in which he was most often found, and where he was almost always welcome. (He had, at one time or another, been barred by every pub in Dublin.) I'm thinking now of McDaid's in Harry Street, which is little more than one room with a very high ceiling. This has been the rendezvous for the *avant garde* in Dublin for years. If ear-rings for men were to become fashionable tomorrow, you'd see the first of them in McDaid's. Here are the corduroy trousers, the sandals, the lurid shirts, the beard, the long hair and the choir of soloists.

When you come in at night, the first impression you get is that everyone is terribly excited about something. You'd be right, for everybody here is excited – by the sound of their own voices, and almost everybody is speaking for effect. Too poor to buy books, nevertheless the customers here discuss the latest books with impressive authority, as they tear plays and films to pieces, and talk also about TV and radio, the chorus is deafening.

Into this used to come, roaring like a bull into an aviary, the

146

gross bulk of Brendan. Through this gliogarumgliog his voice projected and dominated. I never heard him speak softly in his life. Everything he sang or said was at double forte and there is many an unprintable account of conversations which he sustained across the width of a street. Here in McDaid's was the company he liked most . . . young, quick-tongued, careless of authority and contemptuous of sacred cows, living from day to day, and living every minute. In their company Brendan felt his leadership in letters, and here his increasing arrogance was rarely challenged. When it was, you heard some remarkable name dropping. It was always surprising to hear, issuing from such an uncouth face, a reference to Proust or Yeats, or hear some idiom in Irish that was as fresh as a mackerel taken from the Connemara sea.

If you still want to walk Brendan Behan's via dolorosa then you'd better have a look at the Bailey in Duke Street which has just now put on a new and shining face. John Ryan, the landlord, bought the place for a song, and part of the purchase price was the goodwill of the ghosts of such people as Arthur Griffith and Oliver St. John Gogarty; and the physical (and occasional) presence of Brendan Behan. Now it must be understood, since you may not be in a position to physically check the veracity of every word I'm writing, that the Bailey is opposite Davy Byrne's. Don't get the ghost of Joyce mixed up with that of Behan.

Brendan, whose hunger for life was such that I suspect he was bisexual, preferred the Olde Dublin atmosphere of the Bailey, rather than the Cafe Royal plushy atmosphere of Davy Byrne's.

Of course he was thrown out of both, several times, but much more often out of the Bailey, because he enjoyed the Bailey more. There were the old photographs of old Dublin city on the walls, and open fireplaces, and a marble counter . . . and you felt here in communion with the good talkers and drinkers of the middle distance past of Dublin.

There was no attempt at disguising the pub, no false ceilings, and masked lights, no taped music and no telephones over which you could not be overheard. Brendan was reasonably happy here, and had enough confidence to turn his back to the door when he was at the bar. The new Bailey, opened recently, would have charmed Brendan who, having orated there once, would have moved on . . . to another of his favourite haunts . . . The Brazen Head in Winetavern Street.

The Brazen Head is the kind of pub that such suave hoteliers as Ken Besson or Toddie O'Sullivan would like to buy. It's so different from the Russell or the Hibernian or the Gresham. Provided that it's after dark, your first entry into the little court-

Brazen Head

yard in Winetavern Street is alluring, and as for the smokey
stoop-your-head bar itself, with its scrambled piano and shiny
plush chairs and general air of genteel neglect, you get, right
away, a bucket full of what is called atmosphere.

'If' (you who has travelled say), 'if they whitewashed the
courtyard walls and put out window boxes full of geraniums and

lobelia and hung a few lanterns here and there . . . then it would be just like that little place you discovered in Paris, or was it Torremolinos, or Kinsale?'

That's if your first visit is after dark, and you have dined well.

Bould Robert Emmet, the darlin' of Eireann, sat and planned here, they say, and that takes you back to 1803. The atmosphere in The Brazen Head about eleven at night feels as though it has been preserved since then, for the tiny little place is stifling and packed with student drinkers. The only thing you can't buy here is oxygen.

When, some years ago, Louis Elliman, the Lord Killanin, Bing Crosby and Walt Disney combined to make one of those whimsy films in which Bing would have to sing in an Irish pub, I was asked to suggest the setting. In a stately procession led by a Rolls Bentley followed by an Austin Princess, I led the nose-quivering party to The Brazen Head, and as we entered the courtyard, we heard the sound of music. A good baritone was singing 'Mother Machree'. But when we tip-toed in and saw the singer, even Hollywood was outfaced. For the singer was a Civic Guard . . . in uniform. There was clearly no need for the film.

Brendan Behan loved this place ... but it was too small for him and it closed too early for him.

Now walk behind the shapeless baggy ghost to Mulligan's in Poolbeg Street, where the dockers and truck drivers from the Port of Dublin congregate. The pint here is classical, and though the Guinness people maintain that every pint, everywhere, is just the same, just try one in Mulligan's and you'll get the message.

Mulligan's is tobacco and mahogany coloured, and they even have gas lamps there yet. The gas lamps there really work. There are framed silken theatre programmes from the old Theatre Royal announcing Vice-Regal occasions in the days when little Johnny Cassidy was knocking at the door, and there's a great old grandfather clock and, in winter time, an open fire that would roast an ox. The dockers who call in there every evening after their day's work are of remarkable physique, earn remarkably good money, and develop each day, remarkable thirsts. Indeed one of the regulars told me that he sometimes drinks twenty pints of stout in one day, and I have no reason to doubt him. In a voice that made a sound like a train going over a bridge, this genial truck driver sang for me 'Play in your own back yard' . . . a sentimental ballad with a curious social undertone.

Here are the flattest of Dublin accents, and here Brendan Behan sounded quite at home. For everyone sounded the way he did, and bellowed the way he did, and to some extent looked the way he did. But, in fact, Brendan was never at his ease in Mulligan's, for the dockers regarded the house painter as a dangerous freak and the ugly duckling preferred to walk on, some ten yards away, to the soft voiced haven of The White Horse. That was the message of 'Play in your own back yard'.

It was all this image of the smelly roaring literary Lucifer that made his filmed interview with Eamonn Andrews all the more moving. The most memorable and heart-breaking moment of the film is when the off camera Eamonn asks, 'Are you afraid of dying?'

When I saw his face then, I was not, at that moment, afraid of him any more, for I realised that he too knew and understood. . . .

> *Sceptre and crown must tumble down*
> *And in the dust be equal made*
> *With the poor crooked scythe and spade.*

We journalists have to learn to know our place. The essential difference between the journalist and the writer is that the former writes because clock or the calendar says that he must. But the writer writes because he must, whether at dawn or next year or here and now, urgently, on the back of a court messenger's writ. So there enters the element of envy now . . . for we, the journalists, are subject to discipline and naturally we envy those who are not. We conserve our energies for the daily fight against the clock and the calendar, and we are economical of words and we preserve our talents.

So I envied Brendan Behan as I would a millionaire, as he poured thousands and thousands of words down the sink, threw away hundreds of television and radio programmes unseen and unheard in some pub. Such a waste of genius there was, never recorded, all gone now with the atomic windy belch of ten thousand pints of stout.

I didn't stand at his graveside. I stood several graves away in the long dank Victorian grass nourished by a century of dead Dubliners.

And I heard his panegyric spoken in Irish, English and French and knew in my secret heart that he'd come back to haunt me. In fact he is haunting us all . . . and that's why this book had to be written, as a kind of exorcism.

3

HIS LONDON APPEARANCES

By Donal Foley

THE prostitutes outside Bow Street Police Court called out warmly: 'Come back soon Brendan – Good old Brendan.'

Looking tousled and dishevelled and with a grin as wide as O'Connell Street Brendan bellowed back at the girls:

'I'll be back – don't worry.'

It was one of the promises that he did not keep. But his appearance on July 11th, 1959 at Bow Street will be remembered by those of us who were present. The previous night Brendan Behan, who was then at the height of his popularity in London, was found in a state of coma in Mayfair. As a result the next morning he was charged with being drunk. He arrived from the prison cells looking a little shy and subdued. The London constable read out the charge and the magistrate asked the routine question:

'Anything known?'

There was a quiet titter in court at the absurdity of the question; but the constable was not at all flurried:

'Not in this court,' he replied.

Brendan, a stickler for accuracy in these matters, reminded the magistrate of his sojourns in various prison establishments and then went on to pay his own special tribute to the London police:

'I was given fourteen years for shooting at two coppers but this black eye didn't come from the cops. They were very kind and very civil.'

The magistrate – Clive Burt – ordered him to pay a fine of five shillings and fifteen shillings expenses. Immediately afterwards Brendan left for London Airport. No less than thirty cars manned by Fleet Street reporters joined in the calvacade to the airport. The inevitable stop for refreshment came at a pub on the Great West Road. The landlord seemed a little apprehensive at the strange invasion in the normally quiet period of a Saturday morning. Reporters were falling over themselves to buy the great man a drink. It was not surprising because at this stage Brendan was worth his weight in gold to the Fleet Street newspapers. His play 'The Hostage' was still packing Wyndhams

Theatre and every word he uttered, drunk or sober, was faithfully recorded for posterity. But today Brendan was having some fun at the newspapermen's expense. He spoke entirely in Irish and advised me to cash in on the situation:

'Charge them translation fees,' he chuckled in Irish.

Nobody enjoyed the joke more when he heard me making a bargain for the golden words. It was the only time in my life that Irish proved of any practical value; unfortunately there are only a few Brendan Behans around. Brendan drank three whiskies and two bottles of stout and left London, his four day spree having cost him £150.

Incidentally when another Irish playwright Oscar Wilde appeared in a London Court he was not accorded the affectionate farewells by the prostitutes that were given to Brendan. The prostitutes jeered and cat-called at Wilde in furious fashion, fearful perhaps that Mrs. Warren's profession was in some little danger from the new cults. There could be the explanation that the street girls instinctively sensed Brendan's infinite compassion and anarchic frame of mind.

Brendan was always at home with the down and outs, the wayward and the men of no property. (Although he could quaff champagne with the best of us.) One night in a pub in Victoria in London two young Teddy Boys were told to leave the pub by the landlord who objected to their offensive behaviour. Brendan, who had taken more than one drink himself, followed the boys out and talked to them for about ten minutes on the pavement. At first they told him to 'Eff off Paddy', but by cajolery and sheer charm Brendan succeeded in establishing rapport with them. Eventually Brendan had the pair of Teds back in the pub with the permission of the landlord. Between them they had a bottle of red wine and spent the night roaring with laughter listening to Brendan's stories.

Not all our experience together in pubs were so happy. I remember the evening we were barred in a well known Irish House in London for talking Irish. Brendan loved the language but he never paraded his knowledge of it with other Irish people. On this occasion his only reason for the use of it was that he wanted to borrow some money from me unknown to the other two Irishmen present who had no knowledge of Irish. We began to talk Irish because I had to explain that although I had not got any money there was a possibility of getting a cheque cashed in a nearby tavern. We had to raise our voices a little above the normal din to get our nuances of meaning across to each other. The Head Barman looked at us suspiciously:

'Enough of that now,' he warned.

Neither Brendan nor I took any notice.

'That settles it – ye've 'ad enough drink,' he said with tremendous finality at the same time removing our two pints from the counter.

We protested, Brendan more vehemently than I. But it was to no avail.

We were asked to leave the pub and not to come back. Brendan had the last word:

'I've been barred from pubs for many things but I've never had the distinction before of being barred for talking Irish.'

We both laughed and went across the road to the Cheshire Cheese where Brendan regaled visiting Americans about the literary Doctor Johnson whose house is not far away. He told the story of the cockney who collapsed in the street and his friend rushed up to Doctor Johnson's believing that the great Doctor was a G.P. for that area.

Brendan's impact on London was in many respects greater than in his native city. The occasion when he appeared drunk on B.B.C. television with Malcolm Muggeridge made him into a national hero with the British working class. He became the toast of every Cockney pub overnight. They identified themselves with this rumbustious Irishman who refused to conform to any pattern. To flout B.B.C. conventions in these new far off conventional days was of course something. The morning after the broadcast Brendan was walking up Victoria Street when a Cockney newspaper seller approached him and grabbed his hand enthusiastically:

'You were great, Mr. Behan – I didn't understand a word you said but I didn't know what Mr. Muggeridge said either.'

It was the latter part that tickled Brendan. He was aware of his own lack of articulation that evening but pleased that Mr. Muggeridge's well phrased and well moderated accents meant as little to the Cockney ear.

During the run of 'The Hostage' and 'The Quare Fellow' in London Brendan had a rare time. Some said that his arrivals in London from Dublin were carefully timed with falling attendances at the shows. True or false his visits certainly stepped up interest in the Behan plays. One never knew what to expect from him. One night, sitting with him watching 'The Hostage', I remember his great big body would shake with laughter and he would turn to me, give me a dig in the side and roar 'wasn't that great'. Then at last completely overcome he roared out 'up the rebels'. He began to call out to the players on the stage –

'Are you a member of Equity?' Howard Goorney who played Pat in 'The Hostage' called out.

'No,' says Brendan. 'The N.U.J.'

Brendan was by now completely convulsed with laughter and he kept up a running commentary with the players. The actors improvised their lines and one quipped:

'Brendan didn't write that.'

At this point the play stopped completely, the actors unable to continue because of their own laughter. It was audience participation at its highest level. After the play Brendan took his curtain call with the rest and danced a hornpipe to the great delight of the audience. Need one add that it was impossible to get a seat at 'The Hostage' for many weeks. Brendan remained around and held court nightly at the Salisbury Tavern in Saint Martin's Lane.

His audiences were mostly journalists but Brendan was happy in their company. He was always conscious of the value of publicity and only on rare occasions have I seen him angry at something written about him. One piece which suggested the possibility of his early death angered him particularly. Brendan did not like what he called 'this death lark' at all. This is why perhaps he called himself 'A Catholic after dark'.

Brendan Behan's language could at times be foul, the four letter words of the Dublin streets, of 'Borstal Boy' and the Army. Women present did not matter to him. But if there were children present Brendan was most careful about the words he used. At a *Yorkshire Post* luncheon where there were many children present Brendan, forewarned by his friend Val Iremonger, spoke for nearly an hour without once using any words to which anyone could object. But later when he had finished his speech he could not contain himself any longer:

'Look at that professional Jesus!' he whispered to his companion when a well known editor of a literary magazine passed across the room.

There is a parrot in a garden in Chiswick, the London suburb which owes something of his vocabulary to Brendan Behan. Brendan when he stayed with the Iremongers in this most respectable of suburbs used to pass the parrot every morning on his way to the station and in his friendly manner he would bid the parrot the time of day. A friendship developed. The parrot now has a vocabulary which would shock any Dublin docker and much to his owners' embarrassment he exercises it freely.

When Brendan lived permanently in London for a short period during the early fifties his only income came from articles in newspapers and magazines. His main source was the *Irish Press* to which he contributed a weekly column. The column was in my opinion the best of its kind to appear anywhere at that time. It was racy, anecdotal, uproariously funny and full of acute observation. Brendan wrote it at an amazing speed. One day at three in the afternoon he came into the *Irish Press* office in London where I worked and asked for an advance of twenty guineas on four articles. I consulted the Editor who authorised me to give him the money, provided I got the four articles in advance.

Brendan looked at me as if horror stricken when I told him the situation. I explained firmly that I could not hand over the money without first getting the articles. Brendan did not say much but warned me to have the £20 at seven o'clock that evening. Meanwhile he retired to the sedate quiet of Lincolns Inn Fields with a pencil and a sheaf of paper. He was back promptly at seven with 7,000 words written. He demanded that I should read the articles before I passed him the money.

'If you're going to be so bloody stern you'll do your own job too,' he shouted at me in mock anger. He was in great form as a result of his achievement:

'A good journalist should work against the clock,' he said proudly.

The articles have since appeared in book form and it is incredible to recall that they were written in such a short time. I believe Brendan enjoyed writing more than anything else and it was this infectious quality which gave his column its character. His robust love of life shone through every line he wrote.

The following day Brendan arrived in Fleet Street in the company of an ex-professional boxer – an obvious victim of the free-for-all boxing booths at the old Blackfriars ring. They had spent the morning together in Billingsgate Fish Market where you can get a drink at the crack of dawn if you are on market business. This was easy for Brendan Behan who was an old hand at the Dublin markets. The Billingsgate and Covent Garden porters knew him as well as the Moore Street shawlies.

Brendan had brought his boxer friend along to meet a mutual friend, a pious Irish newspaper executive for whom he had a great affection but whom he also liked to shock. (He rang him on his honeymoon in London to confide that he was in bed with a woman omitting to mention that he had been married the previous day, and that the lady was his wife Beatrice.) But the shocks that day were to come from Brendan's boxer friend. Brendan introduced him as of good Irish Catholic stock. Whereupon the boxer began to talk about the good old days in the most colourfully phrased foul language I have ever heard. The newspaper executive finally remonstrated with him.

'That's strange language for a Catholic.'

The boxer looked at him puzzled and replied:

'I said I was a Catholic not a fanatic.'

Brendan sat there drinking his pint and enjoying every moment of the unusual encounter. His impish sense of fun was satisfied.

Brendan Behan had many good friends in London but he was happiest in the East End particularly in Stratford East near the Theatre Royal where he saw his first big stage success under the hand of Joan Littlewood. Here in the cafes and taverns in the little mean streets Brendan would sit for hours with obscure unlettered Cockneys giving them his wit and listening to their lore. He became an expert at Cockney rhyming slang and dialects. His cockney imitations were pure music hall. Many Londoners have pleasant memories of his ballad singing for he was liable at any moment to burst into song. He did so one particular evening in The Coal Hole public house on the Strand. The house was cleared instantly. A bewildered Brendan found himself unceremoniously bundled on to the pavement.

The Behan first nights at Stratford East were something to remember. The playwright in evening dress which never seemed to fit him properly would greet almost every person present. The party in the long bar at the Theatre Royal would be well under way before the rise of the curtain and the result usually was that a certain anarchic atmosphere prevailed even before the anarchy began on the stage.

The first night of 'The Hostage' attracted the oddest collection of people, there were so many people with beards and unusual dress that one playgoer was heard to remark: 'What's this – the annual meeting of the Explorers' Club?' Ultimately the play began with members of the avant-garde standing all round the walls. It seemed rather appropriate that the first scene should take place in a Dublin brothel. But the play had a lyrical gusto that carried it along and the players helped by their tremendous enthusiasm.

The author came on stage immediately the curtain came down. There was tremendous applause and irreverent shouting before Brendan, his head inclined to one side made himself heard: 'If you want to know what it was all about, you'll have to read my colleagues in the morning. I, myself am a fully paid up member of the National Union of Journalists.' The play was well received by the critics and, as I have said, went on to the West End.

It received the final accolade of approval when Princess Margaret attended a performance. Brendan's reaction to the Royal visit was: 'I knew her husband – a decent youngster. I spent a night with him in Dublin when he came over to take some photographs.'

The Irish middle-class in London did not take kindly to Brendan. They felt that he was reviving the image of the stage Irishman and that he was a disgrace to Ireland. He was often refused entry to the more respectable Irish clubs. Not that he cared much.

Those who knew him well will remember him for what he was. A man of genius and compassion. As he would say himself 'an 'oul softie.' His Governor in Borstal, where he spent formative years of his youth, wrote of him some time ago: 'You may think of him as the genius and the drunkard, but I remember him as a boy of nineteen who wanted to serve God and who loved his mother and his country.'

It is no bad epitaph and it is one that Brendan would have liked. One thing is sure. It will be some time before an Irishman of such colour and wild genius will strike London town. He gave his friends eight years of joy and despair. God rest him.

Emmet Bridge

4

JUST ONE DAY

By Liam Dwyer *

ONE sunny morning I was standing at the corner of Emmet Bridge and the canal bank. The year 1948, the month April. The time 10.25 a.m. A gentle breeze stirring the water and the young leaves on those 'more sinned against than sinning trees'. God's in his heaven, all's right with the world this bright morning. So far.

I am talking to a priest. A parish priest. From the deep south of Ireland. A crafty type of man. No great believer, I guessed, in the honesty of Dublin car-salesmen, or anybody else for that matter, having listened to a lot of confessions in his time. I suppose. However, I'm working on him. He's up here to buy a car and I'm the man to sell him one.

This is the beginning, the preliminary sparring. I had an act for sales resistant priests. It would be laughed at as 'old hat', nowadays, but things always changed rapidly in the car game. There have been more pioneers than Henry Ford.

I would pull out my handkerchief, a rosary beads mixed up with it, and let them fall at His Reverence's feet. It always seemed to help the 'sky' relax a bit, softened him up, like. Two friends of mine had given their opinion on why it worked so well, one a gentle God fearing citizen said it showed the holy priest how devoted I was. The other friend, a budding (or pudding) writer, as he described himself, agreed with me when I said that the Reverend more than likely believed I was a damn fool and therefore honest.

Howandever and for whatever reason it seemed to work.

I was stooping to pick up the beads, having started the act, making to pick them up before the handkerchief of course, to show proper respect and to make sure he didn't miss seeing them, when suddenly out of the calm air of the morning, came a clear and powerful voice, singing not so much to us as at us.

A nursery rhyme. Harmless enough! Sure, but not in this set up. 'See the robbers passing by, passing by, my fair lady.'

* This is an extract from a book which Liam Dwyer is writing and in which Brendan Behan figures prominently. The writer who was known as 'the big fella' to Brendan was described to an English journalist once by Behan as 'the man who invented me'.

The budding genius himself, Brendan, halfway across the road to the pub, stroke of half ten, Sam just opening the door. O lamentable Jazus: Brendan laughing all over his face, laughing at me, laughing at the sky-pilot, his shirt open down to his belly. 'The top of the morning to you,' he says to me. To the priest he adds 'if we'd anything to go with it, father.' His Reverence says to me, very politely mind you, 'I'll have a look around a few other garages and if I can't get anything to suit me I'll call back.' 'Right' says I, and O hell to myself. Into the pub, there's the bloody Brendan. 'Why did you do that, you——?'

'Aw, for Christ's sake,' he says, 'I wanted to get you away from that ould guy this fine and glorious morning. You'd be talking for an hour and I'm damn well dying, and ould Beary, the publican, told Sam to give me no more tick, and anyway, cheer up, God never closes one door but he closes a bloody dozen, and so to hell with the begrudgers.'

The inside of Beary's was a bit like a museum, polished mahogany, glass, marble and a musty smell. Old Beary came in straight from 10 o'clock Mass at Mount Argus. He put a prayer book as big as a loaf on the shelf straight in front of Brendan's bleary bloodshot eyes, and turning looked into my bleary bloodshot mince pies and says, 'Good morning, Mister D.' I had cleared my slate the day before. Brendan, of course, wasn't in such a state of grace. He looks at Brendan and says, 'What about your account?', and Brendan says, still looking at the gilt edged symbol of the Irish Union of Church and business; 'Mister B., the poor shall always be with us.' Old Beary's eyes narrowed, 'That kind of talk won't help to pay my debts, Mr. Behan.' 'No,' says Brendan, 'you're right, in fact there's an old saying among the geezers on this side of the counter, that it takes a lot of talk to fill a pint, but I have prospects, Mr. B., good prospects.' 'Well,' says the old fellow, 'God helps those that helps themselves.' 'It's true I suppose' says Brendan, 'He's also on the side of the big battalions, and one of those old English blokes said, after he'd been certified as mad, mark you, that an honest God was the noblest work of man.'

Beary looked out of the sunlit fanlight through which the Dublin mountains could be seen. I followed his gaze, as they say, and I reckoned he was looking at the distant Hell Fire Club ruins. It was about all he could do, just then.

So we stayed there, and milled a dozen pints between us, until the Holy Hour. He went off down town, I home for grub.

Later that evening he returned with a young Jewish fellow, who needed a car to carry him around collecting his money-

160

lender father's bad debts in tenements in and around Railway Street, Mountjoy Square and such residential areas. He needed a fairly lively machine as he might well have to make many a quick getaway. The financiers of the world have their troubles too.

I sold him a fourth-hand V8. The right tool for the job. During the making of the deal, I dragged out the handkerchief to wipe the remainder of the porter stains off my mouth and the beads fell, a real accident, and Behan said; 'There you are, Isaac, I told you the Big Fella's a decent man. He's religious, a good sign in any man, what matter if he doesn't dig with the same foot as yourself.' The Jew, a decent fellow himself, nodded his curly head and paid me.

We moved in the direction of the house of Beary. Brendan a couple of steps in front. Walking slowly and singing, easily, like Armstrong on about half throttle, 'McHeath spends lak a Sail-AH ——.'

The Jew had been his client. He was in for a cut, a slice.

The Bailey

5

RITE WORDS IN ROTE ORDER

By Gabriel Fallon

I IMAGINE that most people had heard of Brendan Behan long before they met him. At all events that is how it was with me. An in-law who frequented an off-Grafton Street poets' pub assured me that there was a regular in that place – a house painter by trade – of whom Dublin was destined to hear more than somewhat.

A year or so later I had a dinner appointment at the Clarence Hotel with Robert Emmet Ginna (whom I had met a few years previously) and Jan Mili, a distinguished New York photographer, both of whom had come to Dublin to prepare an article for *Life* magazine on Sean O'Casey. For the purposes of this article they were anxious to meet a Dublin writer who might comparably be in the position that O'Casey was in when he submitted his first play to the Abbey Theatre. To this end they had invited Brendan to meet them. They were amazed when I told them I had never met the man.

Two hours overdue Brendan arrived, flanked on each side by a Clarence waiter. It at once occurred to me that this appearance under guard, so to speak, was due to the man's innate shyness, a quality which few in time would account to him for virtue. Even at that moment shyness seemed no part of his make-up for he opened the ball by saying: 'You're bloody Americans, aren't you; you and you, but not you, Gabriel; you're a poor Dublin slob like myself. I'll have none of this effin, coffee lark.' (And turning to his waiter escort) 'What are you going to have boys?' The 'boys' – somewhat hesitantly – named their particular poisons and Brendan clinched the situation saying 'Doubles all round!'

His hosts were delighted with him and so was I, though I privately assured them that their guest had little in common with the puritanical tea-drinking Sean O'Casey. Brendan shortened the evening for us by singing in Irish, English and French, and by convincing us in between that whatever writing he was destined to lay before the world's eyes it would be filled from top to toe with what Henry James called the evidence of 'felt life'.

Late that night, or, rather, early next morning he and I walked

Dublin streets under a soft misty rain. He gave me in outline some of what he was setting down with much greater detail in 'Borstal Boy'. We left each other in the knowledge that apart from being Dubliners we had one great bond in common. He and I had received our primary education at the saintly hands of a very remarkable woman – Sister Monica of the French Sisters of Charity as they were then called. Brendan never removed himself too far from the protection of her white 'cornette'. She figures at least twice in his writings and his brother Dominic has given a vivid picture of her in his 'Teems of Times and Happy Returns'.

Alas, the 'cornette' has gone down in what Brendan would call the 'latest ecclesiastical fashion lark' and no one misses those 'white wings that never grew weary' more than he would have missed them unless perhaps it happens to be myself. Such was my first meeting with Brendan. It was not to be my last.

*

Others have written of that memorable first night of 'The Quare Fellow' at the Pike Theatre when I met Brendan for the second time. He gladly autographed in Irish a programme for an English friend of mine saying that he wouldn't hold his birth-place against him. I was convinced that given health with discipline Brendan had it in him to be another and possibly a greater O'Casey. In my review of the play I said so and promptly received an anonymous letter – obviously from a literary source – telling me that I was talking through my hat. As Brendan's fame spread further afield he was to feel the whips and scorns of Dublin's notorious literary jealousy of which there was not a single iota in his own make-up.

What a different Brendan I was to meet a few months later in the dress-circle of the Abbey-in-Queen's Theatre when 'The Quare Fellow' was given its second Dublin presentation. Here was a posh, pomaded young man, smartly tuxedoed in black and white with a profile like the head on an old Roman coin, sitting proudly between his father and mother. He knew this theatre well. His uncle, the famous P. J. Bourke, had been its lessee for a long period and had presented most of his own melodramas on its stage. In his curtain speech Brendan duly made reference to this fact.

I much preferred the Pike production to this Abbey one which, despite some excellent acting, was completely overcast by a photographic stone-by-stone decor of Mountjoy Prison. In addition, some of Warder Regan's best and most moving speeches had been cut on the grounds that they might give offence. Brendan didn't seem to mind. Whatever the circumstances he was incapable of prideful resentment or of bearing malice.

*

It is inevitable that with such an explosive character as Brendan's one's chronological sense is likely to be bent or twisted. I know that I had seen 'The Hostage' during its Wyndham Theatre run and loved every moment of Joan Littlewood's presentation of it. I had heard that Brendan had offered it to the Abbey Theatre of which I was now a director, no less. Of one thing alone I am certain. When this incident occurred Brendan had just returned from a boisterous inspection of the U.S.A. and Canada. I met him at the corner of Hawkins Street five minutes after the Scotch House had, fortunately or unfortunately, closed for the 'Holy Hour'.

He was wearing a well cut expensive sports jacket with equally expensive pants, was suitably barbered and bore no evidence of recent, riotous living. Having inquired after each other's health and expressed regret at the drawn shutters which prevented us from sitting with well filled glasses between us I asked him if he had 'anything on the stocks'. 'I . . . h-have,' said he, with that slight impediment which invariably affected his speech when sober. 'I . . . I'm . . . workin' on a bloody play.' 'Jay, Ga . . . Gabriel,' he added 'if only a p . . . play consisted of *two* b . . . bloody acts. I suppose that e . . . even you'd be writin' one.'

'Too true, Brendan, I would. But listen to me now. I hope that when you have this new play finished you will give it to the Abbey.' 'Wh . . . Why should I?' he replied, 'after what Earnan (Ernest Blythe) said when I offered him "The Hostage"?' 'Why, what did he say, Brendan?' Then came this magnificent piece of bi-lingualism. 'He said: "*Ta se too-effin-well ro laidir!*"'* It is to Earnan's credit that when I told him he laughed even more heartily than I did.

*

Then there was that first-night at the Gate Theatre of Miss Eve Watkinson's presentation of 'The Way of the World' during the intervals of which Brendan insisted in carrying on a five-seats-away conversation with me to the amusement of some but to the disgust of the bourgeois majority. He insisted first of all in pointing out Miss Watkinson's father whom I knew anyway.

* 'It is too-effin-well strong'

He was the head of the Dublin firm of Panton-Watkinson, painters and decorators, and the point was that Brendan had at one time worked for that firm.

'Met him outside,' said Brendan, this time without impediment. 'Said "Good-evening, Behan"; very posh; Jay, Gabriel, I thought he was goin' to say "Look here, you; put another effin' coat on that radiator!" ' This, believe it or not, is evidence of an existential innocence. Look at Duncan Melvin's excellent photograph of Brendan on the dust-jacket of 'The Quare Fellow' and you will see it peeping through.

He returned to his seat before the end of the final interval and shouted across to me: 'I suppose you and I are the only scholars who know how this effin' jag ends. D'ye know how I happen to know?' I signalled a negative. 'Believe it or not, Gabriel, they have a copy in the library up in the effin' Joy' (Mountjoy Jail).

*

There was the Dublin Theatre Festival symposium (on Dublin's corniest problem 'What's Wrong with the Irish Theatre?') of which I was Chairman at the Rupert Guinness Memorial Hall. Brendan, cheerfully sober, was one of the panel. Quite unexpectedly at least so far as I was concerned, Brendan was bitterly and unfairly attacked by a fellow dramatist who was also a member of the panel. It was obviously an outstanding instance of Dublin's now widely known jealousy. Who wrote Brendan's plays for him, this speaker wished to know and more to the same effect.

When the man had finished Brendan placed his cigar in the ash-tray, took a final mouthful from his glass of soda water, and indicated to me that he wished to speak. It was the only occasion on which I had seen Brendan moved to anger, a slow ice-cold anger, as he calmly tore apart Dublin's literary pretensions and demolished his opponent's statements in a recital of incontrovertible facts. It made one sorry for the original speaker. When it was finished Brendan became his old self again; he never needed the excitation of hard liquor to be jolly good company. The only remark he passed to me afterwards about his attacker was one imbued with all that charity demanded of us by St. Paul. It was what I expected of him.

*

The last meeting of the long-standing and perhaps unfairly-treated Technical Students' Debating Society was held in a top back-room on Parnell Square. The motion was: 'That Brendan Behan is not a worthwhile Irish writer'. As I had been a good friend to the Society in its time they asked me to preside at this their final meeting. Since the subject of the motion was in town it was thought that he might attend. Perhaps as well he didn't.

I had to listen as speaker after speaker gave vent to some of the greatest nationalistic-cum-pietistic bolony yet launched against Brendan, his works and pomps. Only one speaker against the motion approached anywhere near the truth. When it came to my turn to sum up I launched out so deeply in Brendan's praise that next morning an Irish Sunday newspaper thought fit to give its report a special heading 'ABBEY DIRECTOR EULOGISES BEHAN'. About ten o'clock that morning the phone rang. It was Brendan. He told me the editor had phoned him the night before, read my remarks to him, and asked for a comment. 'Well,' he said to the editor, 'it's one thing when a lot of bloody ignorant yahoos praise you up to the skies; it is quite another thing when someone with a little intelligence says a few nice things about you.'

The Editor then read him the anti-Behan speeches, warning him beforehand that he had no intention of printing them. Brendan listened in silence. The Editor then asked him if he had any printable comment to make on the attitude of the speakers. 'I have,' said Brendan, 'if you'll print it.' 'What is it?' asked the Editor. 'Well, here it is in a sentence' said Brendan 'but I don't believe you'll print it: "Crawthumpers of the world unite; you've nothing to lose except your effin' brains!" ' And that was that.

*

That Brendan was a lovable character there is not the slightest doubt. It would be indeed true to say of him that 'he nothing common did or mean' except that he would strenuously object to being coupled with Andrew Marvell's tribute to King Charles I. He was generous beyond measure. Someone rightly said of him that he had a heart as big as the Isle of Man. There was a sense in which Brendan could say with Bernanos '*Je ne suis pas un écrivain*' and mean it. He had none of the artificial elements of composition so prized by the born writer. He loved life even more than he loved literature. I think he would have been content to be described in words taken from 'Finnegan's Wake': 'The ring man in the wrong shop but the rite words in the rote order?' an epitaph, incidentally, that makes him perhaps an even greater writer than at the moment we take him to be.

He had much of the innocence of childhood about him, a rich sense of wonder and a great basic humility. He told millions of television viewers that he was a bad Catholic and he did so with all the earnestness of the Publican in the parable. Many took advantage of him; he was more sinned against than sinning. Like most of us he was afraid of the finger of God. His greatest virtue was integrity. He was what he was, and absolutely. He carried good and evil, each in its place, as he himself might have put it 'so that God can see more quickly where he is on the day of judgement.' And he went from us in the faith of his own Warder Regan in 'The Quare Fellow' with someone holding his hand and 'telling him to lean on God's mercy that was stronger than the power of men'.

PART FOUR

The Behan we Knew

'Did you ever hear the one . . .?' Maybe you have heard some but certainly you haven't heard a fraction of those inimitable Behan anecdotes collected here, in most cases for the first time, by Catherine Rynne. This is a treasury made up by the people who knew him in every walk of life . . . a treasury that links wit, humanity and legendary humour.

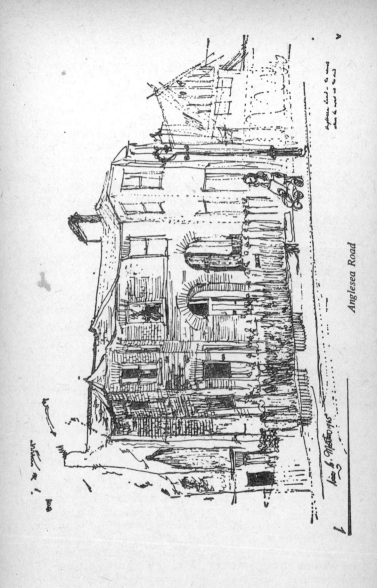

Anglesea Road

THE BEHAN WE KNEW

By Catherine Rynne

SELDOM the hard word for Brendan. Talk to those who knew him and they close in their ranks. Dismiss his faults and underline his virtues. He yelled across streets at them. Called at their houses in the small hours. Annoyed the life out of them betimes. Often embarrassed them hugely.

But he is remembered with affection, 'I was very fond of him,' said one man seriously, 'I would put up with behaviour from him that I wouldn't put up with from anybody else. I was indulgent towards him and put him in a class apart.' He is remembered with laughter, 'I can't think of anything serious about him. It was all fun,' sighed a publican, leaning on his arms to chuckle again over yesterday's crack. He is remembered with respect, 'He was a terribly nice type'. And often with love.

Brendan's friendships ranged indiscriminately through barmen, civil servants, taximen, journalists. The banjo player who walked all the way out to his funeral in Glasnevin. The judge who shared a joke with him. The patriot, scholar, soldier. He tried their adoption. Won their loyalty. Here are some of their reminiscences.

*

Sean Lloyd, aged 70, lives in Russell Street on the second floor of what used to be a Georgian mansion. Across the road is the shell of the house where the Behans lived until Brendan was about twelve. The walls of the Lloyd flat are covered with war mementos, batons, medals and decorations. And the conversation is military:

'I first met him when he was about fourteen and a member of Fianna Eireann. All his life he tried to consolidate the one achievement. He was a rebel from the cradle to the grave. I remember a trip to Bodenstown cemetery, where Wolfe Tone is buried. After the speeches, the I.R.A. and Fianna would meet, congregate, have a drink, have a chat. There'd be rejoicing if there were no arrests. Brendan got into a bit of an argument with the people and the Gardai. He was very revolutionary then. I often looked on him as an outstanding feature of the revolution.'

Anyway, Sean persuaded the sixteen year old ('he'd have had a bottle of stout maybe but he wasn't drunk') to come along home. And he thought none the less of him for his excitability. 'I always admired him. Even as a young boy he presented the soldier-like manner.'

Later, Lloyd and Behan were interned in the Curragh at the same time, the mid 1940's, for anti-Government activities. The prisoners, members of the Fianna and Volunteers, were kept in two sections, nicknamed 'tin town' and 'rat camp', in the former British military camp. Brendan was among a group of six that escaped after five months, while Sean spent nine months 'on the rat'.

The pair met once a fortnight or so. 'What way do you think it is, Sean?' There would be some serious conversation. Then suddenly, 'He'd burst out in old patriotic songs, clap you on the back . . . and he's gone'. The kind of things he sang ranged from 'Lloyd George is in sorrow, he fears for tomorrow' to 'Sinn Feiners pro Germans, Alive, Alive-O' and the 'Sean Bhean Bhoct', or poor old woman, representing Ireland, to whom French aid was coming across the seas.

Although tea and cocoa were rationed, alcohol was out ('You'd miss the old drink', said Brendan once to Sean, 'To hell with it, we'll get over that') and their letters heavily censored, morale among the men seems to have been high: 'We'd come out on early morning exercise and sing ditties. "Stop singing and cut it out", we'd be told.' Failure to obey meant deprival of meals. 'But sometimes we'd get together and decide to let it ring.' Brendan, naturally, was in on the composition of these same derogatory songs. 'I remember him composing them with another fellow and disagreeing about it.'

Subsequent chance meetings with Brendan in various city pubs found him still on the patriotic theme: 'My God, Sean, what have these men died for? What would they think if they came back? Thank God, they've gone. Their memory lives on. But what they died for hasn't come to be.' Of more recent years he didn't comment so much, although he still felt the same way about these things. On one of our last meetings, he said: 'We're still passing out, Sean. We won't see the Republic accomplished in our time, except for a miracle. And it would want to be a miracle.'

*

The ex-borstal boy used to boast that he had been 'in every respectable jail in the world.' Mountjoy was probably high on the list. He got on very well with the governor there, Mr. Sean

172

Kavanagh, who arranged a meeting between the young prisoner and the well known writer, **Sean O'Faolain.**

O'Faolain remembers 'a slim, black curly-haired man. He reminded me of Dylan Thomas in Augustus John's portrait, a quiet, gentle creature. Nothing of the wild man that was to come later. I had been asked by the Governor to pay him a visit, be a sort of paternal visitor. I provided talk, cigarettes, the odd few shillings. And I read his work. He showed me a story he had published in Paris a year or two earlier. It was as subtle and delicate a story as I had read. I read two parts of 'Borstal Boy' and later we published snatches of it in *The Bell*.

'I was surprised at the absence of bitterness in young Behan. It was later the public legend took over and it was hard on the private thing. In every writer is buried a soft gentleness and this I feel would have developed in Brendan if he had lived a wiser life.'

*

In a Victorian house off South Circular Road, Dublin, are two rooms which were painted and papered by Brendan Behan. They still seem to ring with the boy's boastful shout: 'It'll last a hundred years!' Here is a couch where he often sat, both as boisterous guest at long-past parties and, shortly before his death, as a man subdued and aged by illness but still reminiscing about happier youthful days.

House-proud **Mrs. A. V. Martin** swears that she will never redecorate these rooms. She knew Brendan the painter, the nascent literateur, the gay young fellow. The painting job was done in 1947. 'He did it for love,' she explains, 'He loved my husband very much. When he was about sixteen, my husband gave him five pounds because he was Peadar Kearney's nephew. He often used to tell me how delighted he was, how it was the first time he'd felt the crinkle of a new £5 note in his hand.'

When she first met him, she had just been 'soaked for £30' by an unscrupulous tradesman who had agreed to paint the house inside and out, only to clear off with the money. Brendan, a close friend of her son Eamon's, heard about this and came along saying that he was 'trying to redeem the painting and decorating trade by doing a good job.'

But she didn't know it would be free: 'I used to watch him like a hawk. He'd be singing, laughing, telling stories and jokes all the time. He taught me all about painting, undercoating and finishing. I can paint beautifully myself now and I learned it all from Brendan. Every now and again, he'd get a notion to go out and buy a book from one of the barrows in the town. He'd tell me to watch the clock and that he'd be back in half an hour. He kept his word too. Once he got a book for 1s. 6d. "There they are thrown out!", he'd say to me. Every day he'd be bringing in a fresh book. Then he'd be telling me about books by the old English writers. I'm sorry I didn't pay more attention to him now. But I wanted to get the job done. He was more interested in reading than in painting. You couldn't keep him from the books.'

A son of the house joined in the conversation here to remark: 'I remember him with a paint brush in one hand and a bottle of stout in the other. "You'll fall, Brendan," we'd say. But he'd put the bottle down on the trestle (this was when he was painting the ceiling) and go on working and singing.'

Mrs. Martin told me how Brendan used to pick her brains openly: 'He'd be getting me to tell him old yarns of Kilbeggan, where I was brought up. He'd sit in front of me writing in a note-book. Once I heard him telling a story on the wireless with the names of the characters I'd told him about. One day, I was telling him about a terrible wild fellow who was always looking for a fight.

'When we were children, we used to be forbidden to look out the window at him when he was walking down the street roaring for someone to fight him. But afterwards I discovered that there was something very nice about him all the same. After this conversation, Brendan went out laughing to my son Eamon and saying "Your mother's after dissecting me!" '

As the owner of a guest-house, Mrs. Martin remembers with mixed feelings an incident involving her house-painter and some la-di-da English visitors: 'He was pushing the window up and down, making faces in at them and using vile language while they were having a meal. Maybe they were just as amused as he was but they ignored him and went on talking. I was trying to keep the peace between them.

'I was all the time fighting him and correcting him and trying to rear him. But it was more a prayer than anything else when he mentioned the Holy Name. I'm sorry now that I didn't show him more kindness. He used to tease me. He said the statue in the room was "only a bit of clay"; that he had a friend who painted statues all day and was so sick of looking at them that he wouldn't pray in front of one of them for love or money. This shocked me a lot at the time. He told me he'd put me into one of his books. He said he'd say I always had the little rasher, the eggs, the sausages, black puddings and the few bottles of stout lined up

Gardiner Street

for him. I wasn't a bit pleased. I'd been hoping for something more romantic!'

When Brendan had finished the job, 'he used to be coming in all hours of the day and night, by the window if the door was locked, to meet the writers that stayed here. Yes, I was a little annoyed with him at this time.' Parties there and 'Brendan would be singing out at the top of his voice. He couldn't be easy. We'd be afraid the neighbours would complain. Afterwards, he wouldn't leave. Sometimes, he'd stay for a couple of days playing with the children. He loved them.' At this point, one of these young nieces came into the room, 'I remember him all right. We used to be playing ball in the backyard. I was afraid of my life of him. He was real rough!'

Finally, Mrs. Martin described a later encounter with Brendan at the Horse Show, perhaps twelve years since she'd been 'trying to rear him.' He was just back from America at the time: 'He'd changed, looked like a lord, was too grand in himself. He'd lost his old frivolous way and was very superior in himself. I didn't realise how much I'd liked him until I saw him changed so much. I liked him better when he was his old self.'

*

Mrs. Caitlin O'Neill is another housewife who remembers having Brendan doing a painting job for her. Her husband, Seamus, was editor of the Irish language monthly, *Comhar*, for a long time and met him in connection with his contributions to it.

'He was awfully young then and had read a great deal,' Mrs. O'Neill recalls, 'this was in 1948. His interests were reading, writing, talking to people. And he was very interested in the Irish language. He was good-natured, everybody will tell you that. And he was very eager, always eager.' As for the painting – 'He continued to read when he was supposed to be working. He was very proud of his union card but his heart wasn't in the painting. It's a mercy to God he didn't continue with it!'

*

Actor Niall Tobin, now a member of the Radio Eireann repertory company, was a guest at one of the aforementioned Martin parties when 'Brendan arrived wearing only a vest and pants and fairly the worse for wear. He sang his head off all night. I got friendly with him afterwards. Eamon Martin had a flat in Elgin Road and Brendan had a room in the same house for a while, I used to stay occasionally with the Martins there. He was at his best then. His mind was very clear and he was tremendously witty. It was an absolute riot having breakfast with him.'

Tobin and a friend had a flat in Herbert Street which was taken over by Brendan and Beatrice shortly after their marriage: 'We left in rather a hurry and some of our letters used to go to the flat afterwards. You were liable to meet Brendan in Baggot Street or Grafton Street and he'd roar the contents of the circulars and postcards across the street at you.

'I remember I was going to Baldoyle Races one Patrick's Day. Brendan and Beatrice were at the bus stop. They weren't long married at the time. He proceeded to give a running commentary of everything he saw on the journey and he had the whole top of the bus in hysterics the whole way out. Without, I might add, using any words that would bring a blush to the most innocent cheek, as they say.'

Parties given by the Behans are described by Tobin as 'enjoyable and highly civilised.' There was no rowdiness whatever. 'He used to speak Irish to me always if he met me and there was nobody else present. His Irish was not very grammatical but very fluent and every bit as expressive as his English. He usen't to curse at all in Irish.

'He was terribly obliging. If he could use influence or abuse to get something for somebody he would always do it. He hated to think that anybody disliked him but he was very intensely disliked by a lot of people.

'He was very shy and very unsure of himself. He would never ask you directly what you thought of his work but he would fish for compliments now and then. The only change coming into the money made on him was a tendency to name-dropping, particularly American names, usually if he was a bit drunk or that and loosing his hold over the company.

'Once I met Brendan on a Saturday. He asked me to go for a drink with him. At the time, he'd been on soda water for about six months. We went to five or six different pubs; each time he'd say "Come on, let's go somewhere else" because people were coming up to him slapping him on the back and he was getting fed up with it. In one place, a fellow came up and said "Hello, Brendan, never a dull moment." In another place, as soon as the barman saw him he said "Get out, you're not served here." I made enquiries afterwards and I found out that Brendan had never been there in his life. It goes to show that even when he was cold sober, and off the drink altogether, people expected something of him.'

There is a place off Grafton Street called McDaid's. For many years it has been considered one of Dublin's leading literary pubs. It was just beginning to get this name when a young house-painter got into the habit of dropping in there during his lunch-hour. Head barman, **Mr. Paddy O'Brien,** has happy memories of him:

'He first started coming here shortly after he was released from prison in 1945. He was always full of wit. When he was painting the Gaiety Theatre, he used to come down here during the dinner break. He asked if there was any painting we wanted done and offered to paint the toilet because he was short of a couple of bob for a drink.

'So he painted the toilet the next day. At the time, it was Holy Week, I think, he was working on the ceiling of the Gaiety. MacLiammoir and those were on the stage rehearsing a play. Behan used to be roaring and shouting and singing his head off. They implored him to be quiet. He'd be imitating them down here. But he would only yell back at them "Bloody parasites". They had to ask the contractors to put him on an outside painting job.'

Brendan was refused drinks in McDaid's several times, 'He was so noisy and the language was something fierce.' But he never held this against Paddy ('We weren't any the worse friends for it') or the establishment. During one of these times, Paddy was cycling through Herbert Street: 'He was living there then, but I'd forgotten all about it. Suddenly, he appeared in the middle of the road, shouting "If you come down here I'll kill you." So I shouted back that if he didn't get out of the way I'd run him down. Then he invited me into his flat. It was like a newspaper office. The floor was littered with foolscap. He opened a press and took out a few bottles of whiskey. Beatrice came in and said hello to me and asked Brendan was he coming. They were going out, but he left me with the whiskey and the freedom of the flat.'

This type of gesture was typical: when 'The Quare Fellow' was first in the Abbey he promised me tickets. The week went by and I heard nothing from him. So I thought he'd forgotten. But the following morning he called up at my house with the two tickets. He was great company and had a great nature. Bob Hope would only be in the second place to him. All the customers knew him and they all got on very well with him. He was always sought after.

'Two or three leeches got after him when he had money and dragged him around the place in taxis. He'd never have drunk so much only for them. And he did all the spending all the day. He wasn't a good drinker at all. Five pints and he'd have had it, not like the fellows there that can drink all day and still walk out of the door at the end.'

Mr. O'Brien described the Behan of the early days as 'Jovial and full of fun': 'If Brendan stayed a house-painter he'd be still alive. That was the sad part about it. Later, he was a bit bitter, slating everybody from a height. But his language was only bad when he was drunk. He only visited here once a week or so afterwards when he made the big time. He was tied up with a lot of blokes that hung on to him. He was a sick man with the drink and that when he got the money.'

*

Mr. Paddy Tobin, a Dublin taxidriver, knew Brendan from the mid 'forties, when he was in a group of bachelors who drank together in the Tower Bar, Henry Street. In those days, his nickname was actually 'the quare fellow': 'Old Stephen Behan used to be there of a Friday evening and there'd be about five of us with maybe only a pound between us. Brendan would keep nudging him for money, saying "It's all right, Da, I'll be getting a few pounds tomorrow." Stephen often parted with his whole week's wages this way, though it would be under pressure.

'When he came into the money, he stuck by his parents. I remember getting a call to the Bailey once to collect Mrs. Behan. I immediately thought of Beatrice. But when I arrived this woman was outside the Bailey in her bedroom slippers. Then Brendan came and said "Have you met the Ma?" He'd been giving her a meal out.'

There was quite an interval between the drinking days at the Tower and Mr. Tobin's next meeting with 'the quare fellow'. 'I was married in 1953 and I went to live in a house which used to be owned by a friend of Brendan's. My wife and I were shortly back from our honeymoon when one night there was an unmerciful banging on the door. A voice yelled through the letter-box what I thought was "Is there anyone in?" I waited for a minute. Then there was an even worse clatter and the voice yelled "Have you any gin?" I decided that this could only be one man and I said "Come on in, Brendan."

'He was very surprised to see me and was all apologies. But then he had a drink and stayed till around four. He used to visit us late at night like that for about six months, each time coming in and having maybe only one drink, and talking till all hours.

'My brother-in-law, who also has a taxi, was often called out to

179

Brendan's place at 4 o'clock in the morning. Brendan would get in and say "Bring me somewhere where I can get a drink." But he wouldn't be thirsty at all. It would only be an excuse to go somewhere. I discovered afterwards that he couldn't sleep at night. He did most of his work at night, and when he had finished he'd be looking around for something to do.

'He helped every bum and renegade in the city. The trouble was he helped the wrong people. In later years, he used to be going around with a crowd of hoboes and suckers. To tell you the truth, we avoided him then. He was always drunk and the language was desperate.'

*

The singing house-painter crops up once more in the memories of Sean O hEigeartaigh, principal of the Department of Finance, and managing director of the Irish language publishing firm, Sairseal agus Dill: 'He was working for Dockrell's at the time and was doing a painting job here in Government Buildings. He sang ballads the whole time, mostly in English though an odd one was in Irish. Yes, it was quite a distraction all right. But we didn't mind.' Brendan was stationed in an enclosed, narrow courtyard, making excellent acoustics for his powerful voice, which wafted up past the windows of scores of civil servants at their desks.

'While I was director of *Comhar*, he used to submit the odd poem and occasional article. He used to drop in periodically and talk to anybody who was there. His articles were interesting. He always had something to say and he said it in an arresting fashion. But I wouldn't describe them as literature. His poems were uneven. He wrote about twenty all told. Some are as good as anything that has been written in modern Irish. There are two excellent ones in our anthology of Irish verse, "Nuabhearsaiocht".

'He suggested a book in Irish about his I.R.A. and prison reminiscences. He came to discuss it with me. He said that he didn't know if his Irish was good enough. He had very fluent Dublin Irish, not perhaps very pure but very effective. So he spent three months in Aran, paid by us as an advance against the book. We gave him £4 a week or so.

'When he was setting off we stepped this up a bit because of the railway fares and the expense of settling in. But he came in and said he wanted more. Knowing Brendan as I did, I wasn't too keen to do this but I gave him a little extra. I heard afterwards that he was seen in the Hibernian Hotel having a meal with a large bottle of wine in front of him!'

After the three months, Brendan wanted to stay on so a scholarship for a further three months was negotiated for him by Mr. O hEigeartaigh from Comhdhail Naisiunta na Gaeilge. 'He sent us drafts of a few chapters from Aran and we sent them back. That was all we ever saw of the book. Certainly he must have written quite a considerable amount of it. We used to chivvy him about it and keep after him. We used to ring him up and ask "What about the book?"

'I don't think he improved his Irish very much in Aran. He spent his time talking, teaching the Aran men Irish, so that they were picking up his idioms instead of vice versa.

'Then he published "Borstal Boy" which contained a lot of material belonging in principle to this Irish book. He offered to write a novel for us based on life in Dublin in the 'twenties. But it never materialised, though we said we would take it. He offered us his play in Irish, "An Giall". We said we'd be delighted to publish it, but not as a substitute for the other book.'

In those days, Brendan was a frequent visitor at Government Buildings: 'He was well known at the enquiry desk. And he'd talk on the phone for hours, interfering with official business. He would tell me all the magazines he was contributing to, such as *Envoy*, *Points* and *Horizons*. He was very keen to hear what you thought of his latest poem. He was a very humble person, would argue a point with you all right but would accept your criticism as valid. He had a genuine interest in the Irish language and was keen to see it advance. Once I was engaged in a controversy about Irish writers in The *Irish Times* and Brendan chipped in to give me a hand. This was part of his patriotism. After all he went to jail for it. One of his favourite modes of address in Irish was "Eist Liomsa" ("Listen to me") and then you had to "eist" all right.'

Mr. O hEigeartaigh remembered a newspaper symposium on where various well known people were going for their holidays: a designer was heading for the Caribbean, an actor for the South of France. But Brendan Behan was going to Carraroe: 'He used to take a house there and so used we. I remember having a long discussion once with him on a rock. He was a tremendous swimmer and used to spend half an hour in the water. He was very popular with his neighbours there. He did no work while he was in Carraroe, as far as I'm aware. And generally he didn't drink much, though he used to go off on spells. If he got into a pub for one reason or another he was liable to stay until it closed.

'Another thing I noticed about him was his love for children. He would talk to my young children in Carraroe, tell them stories

181

of what he was doing, wheel them around.' Of later years, with money and fame, 'as far as I was concerned he didn't change. He was still the same frank, uninhibited, friendly Brendan.'

*

Sean Murphy, owner of an old pub generally referred to as the Hive, in Powerscourt, Dublin, also knew Brendan from the mid 'forties: 'One day an old fellow was asking him was he Mr. Breen. Brendan guessed who he meant: "Oh, do you mean Behan. I know him but he's a right louser!" What he didn't say about himself that day wasn't worth saying.

'One of his favourite expressions was "Anybody could be a success for a day". I think it applied very much to him. He was very well behaved always in here because he hadn't an audience. Once, at the time the Hungarian refugees were being brought into Ireland, he came in one morning. "What's this I hear about the Hungarians?" he asked me. Playing safe, I just said that they were here. "And is it true that they're still trying to get the tinkers out of Ballyfermot?" I said it was. "Well, we're a great — country," he shouted, "welcoming the refugees from Hungary and chasing the tinkers out of Ballyfermot!"

'A taximan I know was always very tidy, not a hair out of place. One day, he brought Brendan to the Gaiety and he asked him would he not button up his shirt. "I can't get a shirt to fit me anywhere," he said, "if it buttons at the neck it comes down to me ankles."

'There was a retired R.U.C. man who used to come in here. Although Brendan fought to free the Six Counties, he would be behaving when he was talking to this old fellow as if he wanted a wall built around them to prevent anyone getting out. He would be going on like that until your man was ready to choke him. Then he'd say that it wasn't anything personal, that he hadn't been thinking he was from the North at all. But a few minutes later he'd be off again.'

*

Mr. Ernest Blythe, managing director of the Abbey Theatre, had an unorthodox introduction to Brendan when the latter was just starting his literary career: 'The first time I met him was when I happened to go into a room in the Abbey and find this young man there using it as an office. This was in the old Abbey after the fire. He had all his papers spread out and has made it his town office. Apparently, someone had told him where the key

182

LIAM G. MARTIN.

WINETAVERN STREET

Winetavern Street

was kept and he had been using it for months. He probably slipped up by the booking office when nobody was looking. He was a bit of a rogue all the time, not a stiff dignified kind of person at all. Anyway, I told him that he could stay there for that day, and afterwards I saw to it that the key was hung somewhere else.

'The next time I saw him I accidentally met him in the street. He denounced Radio Eireann and the B.B.C. because they had rejected a play of his. He said it was good and cursed them up and down. This play contained the germ and the climax of "The Quare Fellow". It just dealt with the coming of the hangman to the jail. It was a lovely little thing, written for the radio, of course, and would have lasted about half an hour. Lennox Robinson liked it. He said it would be easy to devise for the stage with very little writing, and that it didn't need to be radically changed. I wrote all this to Brendan and didn't hear anything from him for about two years.

'Then he sent me a bloated version of the play, which would have lasted from eight to midnight. We sent it back and asked him to reduce it by about half the length. We heard no more for a while. Apparently, he hawked around this bloated version to everybody until finally Mrs. Alan Simpson took it, cut yards out of it and wrote what she wanted in other scenes, for him to fill in with dialogue. After the Pike production he rang to say that the play was now short. He paid an early morning visit to my house and dropped it in for me to read. I passed it round the other directors and sent out the contract to Brendan. An hour after he received it, a messenger was over for the £30 due to him.'

It was then that the trouble started. No sooner had the Abbey put a notice outside announcing the forthcoming play than the Simpsons were in to Mr. Blythe to say that they had the rights of 'The Quare Fellow'. They only had a verbal contract and the cheque of £25 from their bank which they had paid the author. So all the Abbey could do for them was acknowledge in their programme the help they had given in the shaping of the work. Next, Radio Eireann gave notice that they were going to produce the play too. They had to be sent a solicitor's letter stating that the Abbey had the rights for a year. It transpired that they also had paid Brendan.

Unperturbed by this confusion, the author 'expressed himself satisfied with the production and so on. He was always open, a bit off-hand, and he didn't care too much. He readily agreed to proposals made here about his play. They may not have been the best but they were reasonable, changes in timing and that kind of thing. He was good natured and pleasant, didn't mind you disagreeing with him.

.'During performances, he used to be sober but was standing endless drinks in the bar. He had a very loud voice and used to be shouting and banging on the counter. But I didn't mind that because I regarded it as another aspect of the entertainment for the people. One night he was standing at the back of the dress circle talking and making comments and causing a disturbance. We sent one of our staff out to him, a very gentle person but firm. She beckoned him outside and gave him a terrible dressing down, telling him that it was disgraceful and that he should be ashamed of himself. He was scared of her ever after and ran away whenever he saw her coming!

'Of later years, I didn't see much of him at all. Once, though he took a taxi at Amiens Street. He was falling asleep and couldn't tell the taximan clearly enough where he wanted to go. So the taximan called at the Abbey to enquire where he'd take him. I remember being amused by this at the time.'

Of Brendan's work, Mr. Blythe commented: 'He had a great deal of talent, was exuberant, over-wrote. He had an original mind and outlook that the ordinary person wouldn't have. For example, when he was taxed with being drunk on television he retorted: "What about it? I wasn't drunk at Mass." He had imagination but lack of restraint. He spread himself. He had no discipline, no sense of form. I think what he most needed was a collaborator. If he had lived I don't know if he would ever have become a first-rate writer. But he could have produced good work if only he had had somebody to cut, trim down and keep the thing in bounds.'

*

Brendan as a writing man was perhaps not the easiest to deal with. He believed in cash on the nail rather than discreet cheques afterwards. He often asked for advances on articles that had yet to be composed. But he was received with endless patience by the editorial board of *Comhar*. **Riobaird MacGabhrain,** manager of Gael Linn, describes these days: 'I got to know him through *Comhar*. I became editor in 1951, having come up to Dublin from Cork University. The friendly relationship between him and the magazine was established at that time. We had an office in Westmoreland Street, just one room at the top of the house. He used to call in regularly.

'You could never be in any doubt as to who was coming. You would hear him singing at the bottom of the stairs, stopping on the way to talk to anyone he'd meet, then singing again. He'd burst in the door. At this time he had no regular source of income. He would come into *Comhar* to see if he could be paid an advance on something to come. I used to help him like that any time I could, even personally. He knew the *Comhar* office was one place where he wouldn't be turned away and he appreciated this.

'Anytime he called in, we'd always go out to the nearest pub and have a drink because with only one room it was hard to talk over anything privately. The *Comhar* people stood the drinks. But when he began to write for the *Irish Press* he would ring up and ask us out for a drink whenever he had a cheque in. He did this to even things up for any drinks he got from us when he was low.

'In 1951, I was thrashing around for something he could write and suggested the I.R.A. days. So he did a series of articles for us on these experiences. This was the first time he wrote on the subject, which afterwards formed the basis of "Borstal Boy". These articles were very live and readable. In one issue we thought there were certain inaccuracies in Brendan's memories and wrote another article on the I.R.A. to go with them. He didn't object and it didn't make all that much difference. It was the vitality in them that mattered, not the factual information.

'When he was writing prose for us, we would often pay him beforehand for articles. We would give him advances and he would promise us the copy on a certain date. If he couldn't give it to us then, he would ring to say when he could. And he would stick to that date. He wasn't a newspaper journalist at all this time, yet he had this mental habit of keeping to deadlines.'

Gael Linn was established in 1953. This meant a move for the *Comhar* staff to more spacious premises in Kildare Street: 'He used to burst in there too, not bothering too much about receptionists. He was a great man for using the phone. As soon as he got in he would ring three or four people. He did a good deal of his own personal writing too on the office typewriters. He would be singing, shouting, keeping up a running commentary all the time. But two hours later the article would be finished and he would go off down to the *Irish Press* with it, no doubt hoping to get his cheque immediately.'

The Damer, a little theatre for the production of plays in Irish, was set up by Gael Linn in 1956. Any time Mr. Mac-Gabhrain met Brendan after this he asked him to write them a play: 'At first he was evasive. Then he said "Maybe, we'll talk about it sometime." Finally, he promised to ring me up about it. One day in McDaid's he said he'd write "An Giall". We made an agreement with him to cover the original version, leaving him free to translate it afterwards.

'He wasn't able to meet the deadline regarding the play. He went to Spain and wrote a lot of it there. Eventually, he met every payment with an instalment, so that it came in bit by bit. Sometimes, he'd be out drinking with a friend and he'd come in looking for a pound. Other times you might meet him in the street and he'd ask you for five or ten shillings. It wasn't easy giving him money like that. Yet he always had the complete check of it in his mind, and never claimed more. He was scattered and haphazard but he had his head soundly screwed on in this respect.'

Brendan always intended translating 'An Giall' and having it produced abroad. It would have been easier for him to write it in English in the first place. But he liked writing in Irish. He was interested in making money at that particular time and he was asked to do this play for the Damer. Also, he felt a sense of gratitude to *Comhar*. He used to say that before he was known at all two magazines always stood by him: *Comhar* and a French magazine called *Points*.

So, in June 1958, 'An Giall' opened in the Damer. It ran for a fortnight, the routine run at the time, and caused no great furore. Later, as 'The Hostage', it became more famous. Brendan's sister-in-law, Celia Salkeld, played the female lead, and the producer was Frank Dermody. 'He thought he was one of the best producers in these islands. He felt that he subdued the play more than he would have done, but later when he saw the audience's reaction he was delighted. He was very pleased and thrilled about the whole thing. Didn't make any effort to have alterations. He had his usual way of bursting into rehearsals, but he didn't stay too long.'

Mr. MacGabhrain had this to say about Brendan as a writer in Irish: 'He was very fond of Irish and enjoyed writing it. He had no great difficulty, because he wrote as he spoke. It was not terribly grammatical, but he infused the same vitality into Irish as he infused into any language he wrote. If he was drinking with friends and in that sort of humour he'd want assurance that he wrote Irish well.'

*

Another office where Brendan was a frequent caller was that of the magazine in Grafton Street. His friend, Garry McElligott, was assistant editor here and made him welcome. Another man on the staff, however, got extremely tired of this daily intrusion and attempted to put an end to it by ordering that the office door should be locked. All those arriving had to knock and announce themselves beforehand, to make sure that they weren't Brendan. This arrangement proved so awkward that it was dropped after a week or so.

Garry, who is now a feature writer with the *R.T.V. Guide*, reminisced about those days in the mid 1950's: 'He was completely uninhibited. You could be walking down Grafton Street with an important business friend whom you wanted to impress when suddenly you would get a stream of friendly foul abuse from the other side of the street. It would be Brendan, down on his knees, shouting under a horse's belly.

'He never forgot anything you did for him. When he came into the money himself he was tremendously generous. There was a scaffolder who had always been very good to Brendan. After the success of 'The Quare Fellow' Brendan was in Synott's pub one morning when this man came in. Things were fairly bad with him then and he was having a job surviving. Brendan asked him how much he would need to meet his contracts, and he answered £250. Brendan excused himself for a moment and came back shortly with the money, putting it down in cash on the counter.'

Another instance of this generosity occurred one morning around 7.30 in The White Horse: 'He arrived with two fellows carrying small attache cases. They were ex-political prisoners from the North of Ireland. He didn't know them at all but they had gone up to him in the street. He bought three or four large drinks for them. When they said they were going, he cleared out his pockets for them, gave them £5 or £6. Then he had to borrow a pound from me to buy a drink for himself!

'The last time he came from England, he got off the boat with a fellow in Spanish uniform of the 1820's, long blue coat and black sombrero. This was an Irish actor and writer whom he'd been on a booze up with in London. He insisted that he should come back to Dublin with him. He had no clothes so Brendan took him to the theatre and got him fitted out from the wardrobe. He stayed with the Behans for three or four weeks until Beatrice lost her patience.'

One of the few occasions when Garry saw Behan really angry without being drunk was when a colleague at the office joked him for wearing a tie, saying ' "The next time you'll be in striped trousers!" He wanted to know why he shouldn't. This hurt his pride. He was extremely sensitive basically and would have liked to have been respectable. He had established himself as a character in Dublin before he became a writer and they wouldn't let him away with it.'

But Brendan sometimes refused to live up to his image. An *Irish Times* journalist described him to John Huston, the film director, as the typical wild Irishman. So he was invited to a party by John: 'There were a lot of Americans there waiting to see him. He walked in immaculate, for the first time in his life respectable. He knew what they expected and decided not to give it to them.

'One day he called into the *Irish Times* office very drunk. He was left there to rest while there was nobody else in the room. When the staff got back there was no sign of Brendan. Or of the newspaper's library. He had carted it all off and sold it at a nearby second-hand bookshop!

'He was extremely fond of kids. They called him Uncle Brendan. There was a childishness behind the so called crudity, and kids adored him. Behan was a very lonely person. He had to be surrounded by people. When he was visiting friends and sleeping in a room by himself he often used to get up in the middle of the night and crawl into bed with the children. He couldn't bear to be alone and this was one of the reasons he drank so much.

'He had great sympathy with writers, with people prepared to give up security to write. He was very proud of the fact that he was one of the few professional writers in the country.'

Garry described Brendan's last days: 'Shortly before his death, he was in a kind of a trance. He used to vanish for days at a time, going to stay with hangers-on. He would give one particular friend his money to hold for him and all the drinks would be paid for out of that. He'd have a taxi for the day and booze all the time. He would be doing away with £50 a day. The fellows would hold on to some of the money. The following morning he would give out a new issue. The trouble was he never could, never even wanted to shake off the people he'd known in the old days. He remained very loyal to them and of course they used him. He was fabulously generous.'

And he received a little generosity in return. One friend 'used to knock around with the crowd but it wasn't for the drinks but in order to try to help Brendan.' A taximan 'had a great love for him. He drove him around all day and never took more than thirty shillings from him.' A fireman 'was very fond of him and looked after him a great deal. It wasn't unusual for him to run him home in an ambulance if he found him drunk at the end of the day.'

*

Michael O'Connell a quiet Limerickman nicknamed 'the boss', who owns The White Horse bar near Burgh Quay, Dublin, was a staunch friend of Brendan's: 'When he started coming to this place first, I used to be afraid that people who didn't know him would take a poor view of having him on the premises. You'd give him a penny if you met him in the street. He had neither clothes nor shoes. He was worse than any of the tramps you'd meet. In later years, he came in one night before "The Quare Fellow" went on in the Abbey and he had a dress suit and the whole lot.

'He was always reasonably well conducted. He never gave me any trouble or caused any rows. I had only to say "Take it easy" and after that I had no trouble. He might be inclined to be a bit rough at times but I knew how to handle him. I was often good to him. He was always very honourable, never asked for the loan of money, just for a couple of drinks now and again if he was short. And he always paid for them afterwards.

'I never had to refuse him a drink, even though sometimes he was fairly well on. He wasn't the kind of fellow who wanted to fall around on the floor. When he'd had enough he went about his business. In the last three or four years, he often used to be on soda water for six months at a time. Then he'd break out. He never complained, never once said anything about his health. He was always in good form and great company up to a point. He never caused me one moment's anxiety. I liked to see him coming in. The crowd in there used to be in stretches on the floor with him. He was a scream altogether in the early days.'

Michael can claim to be one of the first in Dublin to know of Brendan's marriage. One spring day 'he came in here with Beatrice and they had two cases with them. He asked me to give him £30 change in English notes. "Are you going travelling?" I asked. "Yes, we're off on our honeymoon" was the reply, "Get me a taxi over to the boat at 7.30. I'll send you a card from Paris!" At first I wasn't inclined to believe it. To tell you the truth, I didn't think there was a woman born who would have him.

'When he was sober, he was the nicest fellow you could meet. He never used bad language then. Even when he had lashings of money, he never did anything wild. He would just buy his round the same as anyone. People would often come up to him and offer him drinks and that kind of thing. They'd be Dublin business and professional men who wanted to boast about it afterwards. He'd be quick enough to tell them what they could do. He wanted no messing over anybody. He never had any time

Michael O'Connell

for anybody joining him that he didn't know. He'd stay in his own company.

'Once he and a friend were having a bit of a batter. When the pubs were shut, they went off together in a taxi and Brendan told him that he'd be spending the night in his house. The next morning, Brendan woke up the friend's children, put them kneeling around his bed, and himself at the foot of it, and got them to say together: "Our father, who art in bed, for heaven's sake get up quickly and bring Brendan over to the Markets for a curer for his head."

'In the early days, Beatrice would be with him nine times out of ten. Latterly, she usen't to be so much with him. I suppose she hadn't the same control as she had in the early stages. He was always very nice to her no matter what state he'd be in.

'Five or six weeks before his last term in hospital, he and Beatrice were here with some English fellows and they had a great session. Then the others left and he was starting to fall asleep. Beatrice was trying to get him to go and he wouldn't leave. Finally, she said she'd have to go herself. But I told her she couldn't leave Brendan here because it was getting on for 2.30. So I got a taxi for him and told him to go home with his wife and have some food, that he'd been drinking enough. He linked his arm in mine and went like a lamb. He kissed my hand as he was getting into the taxi.'

A niece of Michael O'Connell's nursed Brendan during one of his spells in hospital. 'She rather liked him, always used to enquire for him. The nurses got great value out of him.' And a son of his, Eddie, entertained Brendan and Beatrice when they were in Los Angeles: 'He often talked afterwards of the great time they had together. He took them to Las Vegas for the day. And one publican who'd never been known to give a free drink in his life took a great fancy to Brendan, gave him a drink every time he went in and made him a present of a bottle of Scotch when he was going.'

*

Mr. Paddy Bolger an employee of the *Irish Press*, says that he had no great liking for Behan the man, though as a writer he couldn't expect to meet any better. The event he remembers best happened once after midnight: 'I was getting a lift home in a police squad car by reason of the fact that I knew a few decent souls in the police station at College Street. As the car swung around College Green there was this figure tottering in the middle of the road, with a hooked thumb imploring for a lift.

It was Brendan and him anchors. The observer in the car turned to the driver and said excitedly: "That was Brendan Behan you just passed." The driver turned on him: "Why didn't you tell me sooner and I'd a run the bastard down." '

*

A Dublin journalist, **Mr. Alec Newman** describes his recollections of Brendan as being 'wholly pleasant ones, and not the least sensational: "An early one was in my office in the *Irish Times*, of which newspaper I was then editor. The office was on a high floor, and overlooked Fleet Street. I had not previously met Brendan when on this occasion we were introduced by my friend and colleague, Bruce Williamson.

'Reasonably enough, our conversation turned on ballads, and all of a sudden, without warning, Brendan said, "Do you know this one?" and forthwith lifted his voice in song. What the ballad was I don't recall: it was certainly both unfamiliar to me and unsuited to the drawing-room.

'This was an exquisite evening in high summer, and the office windows were wide open. "Lord," said my secretary, "would you look out of the window?" The pavement on the opposite side of the narrow Fleet Street was crammed with people, all with their heads craned upwards, and others were hastening from both ends of the street to augment the throng. As Brendan finished, there was an explosion of applause, which he acknowledged with an encore. And, indeed, he would have gone on all night if I hadn't closed the window with the explanation that the work of editing the *Irish Times* had to go on.

'On a later occasion I was proceeding peacefully down the same Fleet Street when a great bellow from the opposite pavement thundered in my ears. "Alec Newman," came the cry, "Alec Newman! Cross the road at once. I wish you to make the acquaintance of my beloved wife, in whom I am well pleased."

'Again, I had boarded a No. 13 bus at Ranelagh. As it was moving off, there came a cry from some yards away: "Alec, Alec, stop the bus!" I did so by means of an imperative jab on the bell. Down the stairs rushed the conductor. "Oh my God", said he, "it's the whole tribe of the Behans. They'll break up the bus."

'There were, in fact, three Behan brothers and two Behan wives, Mrs. Brendan not being of the party. As for the conductor's fears, they were unrealised. A quieter and better-behaved party never occupied the top deck of a bus. Brendan sat beside me and discussed Austin Clarke all the way to the top of Grafton Street.

'Or nearly all the way. "Brendan," said I, as the party was preparing to disembark, "the good Dublin tradition has it that you're never sober after ten a.m." "Don't believe a word of it," said he. "The operative time is the holy hour. Two-and-a-half hours to go yet".'

*

After Brendan's death, his towel and swimming togs had to be thrown out from Tara Street Baths, where he was a fairly regular visitor. Mr. Liam Ellis an attendant, had this to say: 'He never gave us any trouble at all. He was a good swimmer. "Is there many in the pool?" he'd ask before he came in, because he didn't like to go in when there were too many there. In January and February, 1964, he used to be here quite a lot.

'He always came in the mornings and always behaved himself in front of the kids. He was very fond of them. Whenever word got round that it was Brendan they'd gang up around him and he'd give them a couple of pennies or maybe sixpence. He was always very decent with them. They'd follow him out when he was going. They'd shout "Oh, there's Brendan Behan!"

'While dressing himself, he'd be chatting with whoever'd be on the pool. He always liked to have a chat with anybody who was around. Whenever he was in England at a show or that he'd always be bound to tell you about it. He'd be telling you about the carry on over there. When he was finished dressing, he'd hand the attendant the price of a jar.

'He was always very respectable in here, though I heard people saying that at times his language could break stones. He would tell the woman to mind his towel and that he'd be back next morning. Maybe he wouldn't be back for a month. "We missed you, Brendan." "Ah, sure, I'm after being in bloody America." He'd come in here maybe three or four times a week, and then not for months.'

*

Another person who remembers Brendan the swimmer is Lavinia Reddin now Mrs. Dermot McCarthy who was working there as a coach a few years ago: 'It was one of those mornings in the baths when the sun broke through about 12.15. This is always a slack time for the coaches. I was sitting at the edge of the pool doing nothing when I suddenly saw the bould Brendan, purple faced and heavy, in rather scanty black trunks. He was

Mulligan's

talking to the baths attendant.

'Ultimately, he entered the deep pool, swam across to the diving boards and clambered on the lower board to "belly flop" into the water. He repeated this performance several times, and then, to my horror, climbed still higher on the 10 metres board and fell off it, head first, into the pool. He appeared to be enjoying himself tremendously. It was then that I noticed that Beatrice was with him, at a safe distance, like a lonely shadow.

'Finally, Brendan gave up his diving practices, and swam back across the bath and emerged on the bank, shaking himself. Beatrice had disappeared. At this point, I was eating my lunch and, with my mouth full of hard boiled egg, I approached the dripping muse. We talked about what I cannot remember, but I know I enjoyed it all. Brendan's wit, observations and true Dublin idiom were a real pleasure to listen to. The man was full of humanity and a genuine kindliness to all.'

*

Lavinia's father, **Justice Kenneth Reddin** is the author of several novels, including one that has been made into a film called 'On Another Shore'. He too had an encounter with Brendan, though on a more formal occasion.

'I was hearing applications for bail when I noticed this heavy-jowled visitor in Court. I think he was sitting at the solicitors' table, where he shouldn't have been of course. The defendant was a man in the motor trade up on a charge involving dud cheques. Brendan said "Your Honour, I want to go bail in this case. I'm willing to meet any guarantee to be made in money for this man's appearance". I commented that this was a very professional phrase. The judgement given was bail of £100 and one surety of £100.

'I said "But Brendan, are you offering yourself as a 'Hostage' in this case?" He had as big a face as you could ask for and it broke into a smile: "I suppose, Justice Reddin, I can guarantee that my man won't break his bail and depart hence to 'Another Shore'."

'The bail was honoured. Many years earlier, my wife and I were on holidays in Carraroe when Brendan was there too. He could speak Irish very well. He was stout, rosy and insolent looking. Shortly before his death I met Brendan in Dame Street. He looked a dying man. But he greeted me as he always did "Hello Kennett".'

*

Mr. Seamus Byrne a dramatist whose 'Design for a Headstone' and 'Innocent Bystander' have both been produced in the Abbey, knew Brendan well and was very fond of him: 'I remember one of the last times I met him. He looked absolutely wretched. He was well on his way to skin and bone, had lost all his weight. I hadn't seen him for quite a while and he'd changed beyond all recognition. I said "Brendan, how are you?" and he answered, "If they tell us what's true, we're all dying, so why should I complain?"

'Although he has been painted as an absolute blackguard, he wasn't like that at all. He was an extremely nice person. This remark was typical of the kind of Brendan I knew. He must have seen the shock and concern in my face.'

*

Jimmy Hiney is one of the last of Ireland's travelling ballad writers. His name is associated with practically every great sporting event in the country, be it a football final, a greyhound coursing classic, or just an anniversary. For each, he has a ballad to mark the occasion. He is a friend of most of the country's writers, and one of these was Brendan. He remembers two funerals.

'One day, a few years ago, I went to the funeral of Lord Longford at Mount Jerome outside Dublin. And there with the hundreds of mourners was Brendan. Dressed in his best he was, fine suit, black tie and all. He sees me and comes up to me, no doubt wondering if we should go into the Protestant Church or not. Or anyway wondering if I would go in. He looked down at me and one of his curly locks fell over his eyes. "Jimmy", says he, putting a large arm around my shoulders, "Jimmy, I think we'll go in and sing a few hymns for the ould. . . . He has as much chance of heaven as either of us."'

The second funeral was Brendan's. Jimmy has written this account:

'After many great men, writers, poets, painters, singers, there are always the outbursts from the pens of others to pay tribute. We have read many to Brendan Behan. What then is left to be said to really sum up, and why should my poor attempt ever go to print? That the reader will judge for himself.

'It is Saturday afternoon and the crowds are in the grounds of the Meath Hospital. I make my way to the room. I clasp the hand of one of his friends. I try to convey my feeling for this great son of Eireann, this rebel soldier of the young Fianna, this

Dubliner whose pen has left something to the world. I cry unashamedly. My tears are falling and his father looks at me and he says: "He was one of ourselves".

'This is the tribute the great Behan would prefer. This is his father's tribute and it could be put another way, the way a great poet wrote it "To walk with kings nor the common touch". Yes, Behan's pen soared high in the air but his feet never left the ground.

'Monday morning, Glasnevin, they are coming to pay the final farewell. Here again is the story of Brendan, one of so many. I am approached by a street banjo player: "I knew you'd be here, Jimmy. I had to walk". And Barton takes out his not too white hankie and wipes his tears and says "He never passed me. And it was always silver and more often paper cash". And his father's words re-echo: "one of ourselves".

'The last post, the Reveille, a comrade in the struggle of full freedom pays tribute. Then in this spring day we hear a strange language echo to the thousands around the grave. The Behan we took so much for granted is hailed in French by a Bulgarian writer and his father's words are now glorious for us all: "He was one of ourselves".'

*

Sean O'Casey was among the many others who wrote of their sorrow on Brendan's death. His words have as sincere a ring to them as Jimmy's, although the great dramatist did not know him personally:

'I recognise the fine talent he had. One thing Brendan Behan never did was exploit his own talents. He should have settled down and rested and not bothered about running around. You simply can't do this all the time, and he was very much in the same mould as Dylan Thomas.

'There is something peculiar in the Gael or the Celt. When he decides to go along the "primrose path" he runs too quickly. This is what Brendan Behan did. He died too quickly.'

PART FIVE
The End

His grave

A LAST INSTALMENT

By John B. Keane

'When you meet the undertaker
Or the young man from the Pru,
Have a pint with what's left over -
Now I'll say good-bye to you.'

BRENDAN BEHAN

THE above four lines, better than any others, give a whole picture of the Dublin tenements where Brendan Behan first saw the light.

The 'young man from the Pru,' was the collector for the Prudential Insurance Society. He came around every week to collect the instalments on the policy which would bury the 'ould wan'. When the ould wan was dead, the insurance money rarely went to the undertaker. The ould wan was always 'buried dacent' with lashings of booze in case the family would be for ever disgraced in the eyes of their neighbours. The undertaker called weekly for his money after that and the young man from the Pru who was prudent enough to instigate a new policy came hot on his heels.

Behan first came to Listowel, where I live, when I was eighteen. I was in my first year of apprenticeship in a chemist's shop. My immediate superior was a man called Michael Quille who had been acquitted of a murder charge while he was in the I.R.A. He had spent a few years in jail with Behan and the bould Brendan called to pay his respects.

That was in 1949. Brendan's companion was an Irish sprint champion by the name of Tony McInerney. They were on their way to Dunquin in the Dingle Peninsula to spend a few days with Kruger Kavanagh. Both were armed with guns but neither, like myself, had any money.

Michael Quille gave a few pounds to Behan. I borrowed a few bob from my mother and we went to Alphonsus Sheehy's pub where I was to read my poems. I subsequently did and Behan, as Michael Quille reminded me on the night of the premiere of my first successful play, advised me to stop feckin' about with poetry and write dramas about the people I knew.

'Poetry is all right,' Behan said between songs that night, 'but it's all written.'

To give him his due, he read some of the poems in Dublin public houses afterwards, punctuating the phrases with expressions like: 'Now there's a grand shaggin' line!' or: 'Bejazus now, that's nicely put!'

There are a thousand stories about Behan and, no doubt, thousands more in the embryo stages. In his cups, or sober, he was chain lightning and the wit flowed from him like champagne but it didn't flow half as fast as his money. God only knows how much he subscribed to the upkeep of talented touchers, to down-and-outs, to old women and street urchins, to the needy mothers of large families and to friends who increased in relation to his fame. He never turned a deaf ear to a fellow soul in genuine plight.

Once, in a Dublin public house, he was touched for a fiver by a gentleman with a nose for suckers. Behan turned him down curtly.

'I remember a time, Behan,' said the toucher, 'when you hadn't an effin' farthing to your name!'

'That may be,' said Behan, 'but you don't remember it half as well as I do!'

A few years before he died, Behan attacked me in the *Irish Times* because of my attitude towards compulsory Irish. I like Irish and I speak Irish but I never approved of *compulsory* Irish and I still don't although Brendan and I frequently spoke in Irish. The *Times* letter was a scathing one and I replied as best I could, sorry that we should have to differ publicly. A few weeks later the *Times* quoted me at length from an address delivered in Cahir, County Tipperary. In the address I defended melodrama and challenged anyone to define the difference between drama and melodrama. I suggested that critics had made melodrama the poor relation of the legitimate theatre, that they had derided it and held it up as something to be ashamed of. Yet all the great dramatists, with some exceptions of course, were indebted to melodrama for their immortality. I gave Behan's 'The Hostage' as the perfect example.

An hour after the comments appeared, Behan was on the phone.

'Johnny, me darling,' he said, 'that was great this morning!'

'What was great?' I asked.

'Ah, don't be so shaggin' modest', he said. 'What you said in the *Times* of course.' He spoke for nearly an hour and it gave me all I could do to get a word in edgeways. We expanded on the theme of melodrama and the line sizzled when he opened up.

'Are you stewed?' I asked.

'Not a drop!' he exploded, 'as God is my judge.'

202

I reminded him of his attack in the *Times*.

'You're too thin-skinned,' he said. 'Sure if I took notice of my critics, I'd be in Grangegorman long ago.'

Not long after that we were both invited to take part in a debate on the Irish Theatre in the Shelbourne Hotel Ballroom in Dublin. The Abbey Theatre also sent along a spokesman in the shape of one of its finest actors, Ray McAnally. He spoke manfully in defence of the Abbey Theatre which he left shortly afterwards.

At one stage he said that the Abbey paid its authors ten per cent royalties for capacity houses. I interrupted to remind him that all I got for 'Sive' was 7½ per cent. 'It must have played to half-empty houses,' he said, although he knew as well as I did that people were turned away every night. I reminded him of this and suddenly a woman jumped from her seat and berated me for interrupting while somebody else was speaking. She said she was a Kerry woman and was ashamed that any person from Kerry should behave in such a fashion. 'The oul' bitch!' said Brendan, under his breath, 'she doesn't like the truth!' She stood in the aisle and would not be silenced. When I asked her to come on the stage, she refused. 'Well then,' I asked, 'what do you want?'

'I'll tell you exactly,' said Behan in a loud whisper; 'she badly wants a good screw - that's what she wants.'

Seamus Kelly, the *Irish Times* drama critic was chairman on that night but there were no more fireworks. It was no fault of the chairman. The truth was that Behan and I saw eye to eye on most things. There was a little short of £300 taken at the box office. This went to a Dublin charity and, as far as I can remember, Behan added substantially to this sum from his own pocket. We were later heckled by a number of students as we left the hotel. 'You know,' said Behan in a loud clear voice, 'it's getting harder and harder to distinguish between Teddy Boys and students.'

The last time I met Brendan alive was in the foyer of the Ormond Hotel in Ormond Quay, Dublin. It was on the morning of the Kerry v. Dublin Grounds Tournament football encounter. He looked terrible and he was almost drunk when he arrived. My son Billy was with me. Brendan took him by the hand and we headed for the lounge.

'I thought you were in hospital?' I said.

'I was,' he said, 'but I escaped.'

He sat down with Billy on his lap. He had a genuine fondness for all children,

When I called for a drink he demanded a glass of gin. It was no use remonstrating. I thought if we had a drink and a chat I might get him to go back to his bed. He drank the double gin neat and called for another. He drank that neat and, swiftly, called for another. By this time a number of Kerry supporters had gathered around to listen to the conversation. I objected to his having the third gin but he abused me roundly. He put his hand into his waistcoat pocket and gave Billy a pound. There were several other children in the lounge. He called them over to where he sat and presented them with the contents of his pockets.

'I never had any money when I was a child!' he said but he didn't say it as if he were sorry for himself; it was just a statement of fact.

Some admirers pressed more double gins on him, although I asked them not to. When I went to the toilet later, one of these told me to mind my own business; that they were taking Behan with them on a pub-crawl. He challenged me to fight so I hit him and left him there. He didn't show up again. When I returned upstairs to the lounge, Brendan was maudlin and incoherent but he still sat with Billy on his lap.

'Don't drink any more,' Billy said.

'Whatever you say, Bill,' said Brendan, 'but I'll have one more just to wash down the last one!'

A large crowd was now gathered in the lounge. He insulted most of these but he spoke mildly and courteously to the old Kerry footballer who sat at his table. A noisy young man pushed his way through the crowds and pumped Brendan's hand, much against Brendan's will.

'We were in the same Brigade in the I.R.A.,' the young man shouted to all and sundry.

Behan suddenly sobered and took a long, hard look at the newcomer.

'Go, 'long, you bowsie!' he quipped. 'The only brigade you ever saw was the Fire Brigade.'

A few weeks later he was dead.

The I.R.A., like characters out of his plays, marched at either side of his coffin. Two nuns, from his kindergarten days, followed close behind. The gurriers, the bowsies, the ould wans and the chisellers were all there. Respected publicans, wealthy business-men, law men and wanted men, all walked side by side in that last trip to Glasnevin. The Dublin pubs did a roaring trade. Tele-vision cameras whirred and a Frenchman spoke over his grave. He would have enjoyed it all but he would have preferred if the ould wans with the shawls and the down-and-outs with the caps on the sides of their heads were up in front where they belonged, because the Dublin poor were closest to his heart and he never forgot that he was one of them. Never were so many characters gathered together in one place.

It was a scene that only Brendan Behan could create.

THE IMPORTANCE OF BEING BRENDAN

By Micheal MacLiammoir

I CAN never remember my first meeting with Brendan Behan. He was one of those men of powerful personality who yet - in my case at any rate - make no profound impression on the first brief encounter, and who, when one looks back over a period that has vanished forever, seem always to have been there.

It may be that fact, that odd feeling that one has always known him, that accounts for the only astonishing incident of my knowledge of him. For our meetings were seldom and invariably by chance. We never said to each other 'Let us meet tomorrow at such and such a time and dine in such and such a place.' Probably he would not have turned up if we had done this. Anyway I never associated him with dinner, still less with luncheon - there is no attempt in that phrase to get a cheap laugh at the expense of his most expensive weakness - and I never really discovered how much we had or had not in common, how much we would have grown in friendship or in the reverse. We never sought each other out: on the other hand I think we never avoided each other. Certainly I never avoided him, and he always appeared glad when, through this chance or that, our paths crossed.

He bored me only when he was drunk for the beautifully simple reason that people who are drunk always bore me, and contrary to much popular belief he was by no means always drunk. Whether sober or drunk his manners were very beautiful in their way, and even in his Bacchanalian moods he was always good-natured. I think that is what I liked most about Brendan: he was a big man in the sense that he had in his composition no spark or smouldering of *dranntail*, that sour, snarling, embittered, resentful, fang-baring grin for which there is no exact equivalent in the English language and that is so ominously familiar to all of us. He was as generous as he was on occasion violent and unreasonable; and that in itself should be enough to endear him to our hearts.

I suppose it was the Brendan the public chuckled over that I cared about less. I always felt that this side of him would disappear one day and that although, as I wrote at the time, the fact that the mere mention of his name calls forth chuckles and frowns from the more ascetic of theatrical circles as well as from those bar-flies who abound in Dublin as in other places and who

have nothing whatsoever to do with the art of the theatre beyond their gaping pleasure in the easy notoriety it offers (with such frequently disastrous consequences) to its children, is no proof at all that Mr. Behan is not a true native of the House of Harlequin. Indeed, his apparent drawbacks, his boisterous and assertive personality, his flair for notoriety (of a not entirely aesthetic pattern) his easy juggling with the most readily understood quips and cracks of his own town and of his own time, all go to prove that he is. And yet to the more analytical sense, his finer qualities; his warmth and generosity, his tenacity, his zest for life, the absence in him of that bitter begrudging spirit of denial that so often characterises what one might call his 'type' in many another Irish playwright, these things cause one to regret the other, at present more insistent, qualities through which he has been popularised. In other words, I seem to scent in Mr. Behan the writer of a tragedy that will come straight from the depths of his being and in which the easy, the too easy, laughter-getters of the Dublin playboy - the Old Stage Irishman of the Sea, as I think in his latest and most convincing yet still not quite real creation - will not be, perhaps, abandoned, but will take, as they

207

took with the earlier O'Casey, their subordinate and rightful place.

I suppose I have made it clear that we were never bosom friends and that makes my behaviour on a certain night in Australia all the more inexplicable. From the moment of arrival at the airport in Sydney where my tour of 'The Importance of Being Oscar' and 'I Must be Talking to my Friends' began, I had been asked about him and once or twice had made some remark of a lightly snappish nature from the sheer monotony of hearing so many questions on the same subject. One evening, just before my opening performance, there was one of those radio or television interviews inseparable from an actor's life on tour, and for some reason unknown and unexplained I began to talk of Brendan as I had never done in my life. It was very curious. I heard my voice saying things that were perfectly sincere yet that came from a source of which I seemed to know nothing at all: it was as though I were listening to the voice and words of somebody else. When at last the interview was over my manager, Brian Tobin, said to me; 'I never realised before how much you liked and admired Brendan: anybody listening to you tonight would think he was your ideal writer as well as being your dearest friend. What in God's name came over you?'

I could not tell him. I did not understand myself. I still do not understand. All I know was that on the following day the news of Brendan's death was in the newspapers and on every radio in the country. We made careful calculations in the differences of time between Dublin and Sydney. Brendan had died at the moment I was pouring out my panegyric to the air.